THE PRECIOUS METALS PLAYBOOK

YOUR ESSENTIAL GUIDE TO BUYING GOLD & SILVER LIKE A PRO

JAMES W. BUSHNELL

THE PRECIOUS METALS PLAYBOOK

Your Essential Guide to Buying Gold & Silver Like a Pro

Published by Vale Publishing

Florida, United States

DISCLAIMER: This book provides information about precious metals investing. The author and publisher are not providing legal, accounting, or financial advice. Readers should consult qualified professionals before making investment decisions. The publisher disclaims any liability arising from use of this information.

ISBN (paperback): 978-0-9632771-1-4

First Edition: 2026

www.valepublishing.com

PLAYBOOK BONUS

FREE BONUS FOR READERS

PRECIOUS METALS QUICK REFERENCE GUIDE

Download your free one-page PDF summary of the key information from this book—premium ranges, red flags, authentication tests, and buyer types at a glance.

Print it and reference it before every purchase.

Get your free guide:

www.valepublishing.com/playbook-bonus

CHAPTER ONE

WHY YOU NEED THIS GUIDE

With sixty years experience within the precious metals market — starting from a card table on Maxwell Street to a professional in the Florida dealer network — distilled into this guide is the information that every buyer deserves before their first purchase and after.

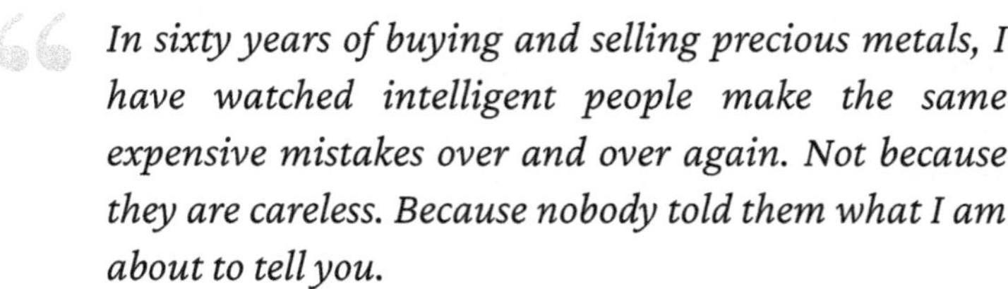

> *In sixty years of buying and selling precious metals, I have watched intelligent people make the same expensive mistakes over and over again. Not because they are careless. Because nobody told them what I am about to tell you.*

Gold and silver have preserved wealth for thousands of years. They have outlasted every paper currency ever printed, survived every empire that tried to replace them with promises, and emerged from every major financial crisis with their purchasing power largely intact. The case for owning precious metals is ancient, well-tested, and as solid as the metals themselves.

Yet the market for buying them is riddled with traps. Television marketers charging twice the fair price for coins that sound impressive but perform poorly. Online dealers that vanish after your wire transfer. Sophisticated counterfeits that fool buyers with decades of experience. Price structures designed to obscure the true cost of every transaction. Storage arrangements that don't hold the metal you think you own.

The gap between the idea of precious metals and the reality of buying them intelligently has cost ordinary people an enormous amount of money. Not because precious metals are a bad investment. But because the knowledge required to navigate this market well is specific, practical, and almost never provided to buyers before they need it.

A MARKET WITHOUT A RULEBOOK

The global precious metals market moves trillions of dollars of value every year. Gold trades on exchanges in London, New York, Shanghai, and Zurich simultaneously. Central banks hold it as a reserve asset. Institutional investors use it to hedge billion-dollar portfolios. Mining companies operate under contracts negotiated months in advance.

None of that directly affects what you pay at a coin shop or an online dealer — but it creates the pricing foundation everything else is built on. Understanding that chain, from global spot price to the coin in your hand, is the first step to knowing whether you are being treated fairly.

The retail precious metals market sits on top of this institutional foundation, and it is a very different environment. Here you find dedicated bullion dealers with tight margins and genuine expertise sitting alongside television marketers with enormous advertising budgets and equally enormous markups. You find online platforms ranging from the scrupulously honest to the openly fraudulent. You find coin shows where genuine bargains and sophisticated fakes appear side by side on adjacent tables.

The retail market has no universal standard of practice. It has no regulatory oversight that protects buyers the way securities law protects stock investors. It rewards buyers who know what they are doing with genuinely good value. It punishes buyers who don't with losses that range from frustrating to devastating.

The precious metals market rewards knowledge and punishes ignorance more consistently than almost any consumer market. The good news is that the knowledge required is finite, practical, and entirely within the reach of any careful person willing to invest the time before investing their money.

SIXTY YEARS, ONE BOOK

I've been in this business for over sixty years. Started on Maxwell Street in Chicago in the late 1950s, selling coins from a card table when I was still a teenager. I've built a shop in Woodstock, Illinois that ran for a decade. Moved to Florida in the nineties and spent years building dealer relationships across the state. I've handled more precious metals transactions than I can count, and I've watched more good people lose money on bad deals than I care to remember.

I've seen gold at thirty-five dollars an ounce and at over five thousand. I've seen silver at four dollars and over one hundred. I've seen the Hunt Brothers corner the silver market and watched it collapse. I've watched the 1980 mania, the 2008 financial crisis surge, the 2011 peak, and the decade of accumulation that followed.

The fundamentals haven't changed. Gold is still gold. Silver is still silver. They've outlasted every paper currency ever printed and every government that tried to replace them with promises.

What has changed is the sophistication of the scams, the complexity of the products being marketed, and the sheer number of ways a buyer who doesn't know what they're doing can lose money before they've taken possession of a single genuine coin.

Tungsten-core counterfeits that fool visual inspection, weight checks, and dimension measurement. Television marketers selling "investment grade" rare coins at enormous premiums to people who wanted simple wealth preservation. Online dealers that vanish with your wire transfer. Storage schemes that don't actually hold the metal you think you own.

Every week I meet someone who made an expensive mistake because they didn't know better. The retired teacher who bought eighty thousand dollars in overpriced numismatic coins thinking she was protecting her savings. The contractor who wired seventeen thousand dollars to an online company that no longer existed when he tried to follow up. The couple who stored silver in their basement in cardboard boxes and lost it to a flood.

These aren't careless people. They're smart, successful individuals who recognized that precious metals made sense for their financial situation. They just didn't have the specific knowledge this market requires.

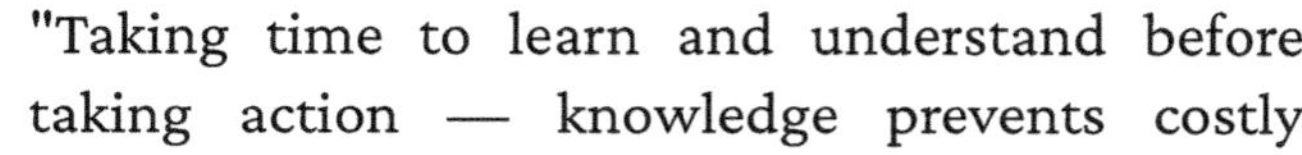

> "Taking time to learn and understand before taking action — knowledge prevents costly

mistakes." Education first. Decisions second. Every time.

WHAT THIS BOOK WILL DO FOR YOU

The precious metals market isn't a mysterious realm accessible only to experts with decades of experience and connections built over a lifetime. It's a real market with real rules — rules that, once you understand them, are straightforward enough that any careful person can navigate them successfully.

You just need to understand the fundamentals. What to buy. Where to buy it. How to verify it's real. What's a fair price. Where to keep it safely. When to buy and when to hold back. How to make sure your family benefits from it when you're gone.

That's what this book covers. Not speculation strategies. Not rare coin collecting. Not get-rich-quick schemes that require you to predict where markets are going. Just the straightforward, practical knowledge that separates the people who do well in precious metals from the people who lose money.

Each chapter is focused on information you can use immediately. By the time you finish, you'll understand the four types of precious metals buyers and which one you are. You'll know which products to buy and which ones exist primarily to separate you from extra money. You'll know how to find legitimate dealers, what fair pricing looks like, how to verify authenticity, how to store what you own securely, and how to approach the question of when to buy without getting caught in the emotional traps that destroy returns.

WHAT THIS BOOK COVERS — CHAPTER BY CHAPTER

1. Chapter 1: The Four Types of Precious Metals Buyers — Which one are you? This determines your entire strategy. Buying the wrong products for your buyer type is the most common and most expensive mistake in this market.
2. Chapter 2: What to Buy (And What to Avoid) — The specific products that make sense for most buyers, and the ones that exist primarily to benefit dealers at your expense. The bullion-versus-numismatic distinction alone will save you thousands.
3. Chapter 3: Where to Buy Without Getting Ripped Off — Local shops, online dealers, coin shows, banks, private sellers. What each option offers, what each one risks, and how to evaluate any dealer before you hand over money.
4. Chapter 4: Pricing Secrets — Premiums, spreads, and the round-trip cost nobody tells you about. Understanding this chapter will save you more money than any other single piece of knowledge in this book.
5. Chapter 5: How to Verify You're Getting Real Metal — From the twenty-dollar magnet test to electronic conductivity testing. The authentication methods that catch what visual inspection misses, including tungsten-core fakes.
6. Chapter 6: Storage, Security & Insurance — The most expensive mistake in precious metals isn't buying fakes or overpaying. It's losing metal you legitimately own to theft, disaster, or because your heirs can't find it.
7. Chapter 7: When to Buy, When to Sell — Why market timing is a fool's errand, how dollar cost averaging removes the guesswork, how to recognize the mania

conditions that signal caution, and how to think about an exit strategy.

A NOTE ON WHAT I'M NOT GOING TO TELL YOU

I'm not going to tell you whether now is a good time to buy precious metals. I don't know, and neither does anyone else, regardless of how confidently they say it.

I'm not going to tell you how high gold or silver is going. I've been in this business for sixty years and I've watched people make and lose fortunes trying to predict those numbers. The market does what the market does, and anyone who tells you they know where it's going is either fooling themselves or trying to sell you something.

What I can tell you is this: the people who have done well in precious metals over the long run aren't the ones who timed it perfectly. They're the ones who understood what they were buying, paid fair prices, verified what they received, stored it properly, and held it for the right reasons without letting emotions drive their decisions.

That's the knowledge in this book. It's unglamorous. It won't make for exciting conversation at dinner parties. But it will save you from the mistakes I've watched cost people real money for sixty years, and it will give you the foundation to build whatever relationship with precious metals actually makes sense for your situation.

The guy with the fake Krugerrand's? He probably hit a dozen more shops after mine before word spread through the dealer network and people started watching for him. Somewhere out there, he found buyers who didn't test.

You won't be one of them.

Let's get started.

★ ***I invest in knowledge and understanding before taking important steps forward — because education is the most valuable asset I own.*** ★

COMING UP NEXT

Chapter One opens with the question experienced dealers use to size up every new customer within the first two minutes: why are you really buying? Most new buyers give the wrong answer — not because they're dishonest, but because they haven't thought it through carefully enough. The right answer changes everything: what products make sense, what prices are worth paying, how long to hold, and how to avoid the traps designed specifically for buyers who haven't asked themselves this question.

Four buyer types. One of them is you. And knowing which one will save you money before you spend a dollar.

CHAPTER TWO

WHAT TO BUY (AND WHAT TO AVOID)

> *The right product for the right buyer. One chapter that will save most people more money than anything else in this book.*

In 1997, about six years after I'd relocated to Florida and was building my dealer network across the state, a woman named Barbara called and asked if I'd look at her precious metals collection. She'd seen my name through a dealer referral and wanted a second opinion on what she owned.

She drove two hours to meet me. That detail mattered — two hours each way to get an opinion she suspected she might not want to hear. That kind of drive tells you something about the person sitting across the table.

When we met, she placed a leather binder on my desk. Inside were certificates for her holdings — professional documents with gold foil seals and engraved borders, the kind of presentation that signals serious money and serious intent. She'd spent eighty thousand dollars building this collection over the previous two years, working with a company she'd found through their television advertisements.

She was a retired school administrator. Widowed. The eighty thousand dollars had come from her late husband's insurance payout. She'd wanted to protect it — not grow it dramatically, just keep it from being eaten by inflation. Precious metals had seemed like the right answer. The company on television had seemed professional and trustworthy.

The company had sold her what they called 'investment grade' rare coins. Walking Liberty half dollars. Morgan silver dollars. Saint-Gardens double eagles. Certified and graded by PCGS and NGC — the two most respected grading services in the numismatic world. The certificates were genuine. The grading was accurate. Everything was exactly what it claimed to be.

I spent an hour going through her collection, looking up recent auction results and dealer wholesale prices on each piece. Barbara sat quietly across from me the whole time, watching my face.

She already knew. People usually do, by the time they drive two hours to ask someone else to confirm it.

Her eighty thousand dollar collection had a current wholesale value of maybe thirty-five thousand dollars. On a very good day, with patient selling to the right collectors over twelve to eighteen months, perhaps forty thousand. She'd paid nearly double what the market would ever pay her back.

> "But they told me these were rare," she said.
> Not angry. Just very tired.

They weren't lying. The coins were graded and certified. They were genuine rare coins. But the company had been selling them at enormous retail markups — charging collectible premiums that far exceeded what most buyers in that market would actually pay. Barbara hadn't bought rare coins at fair market value. She'd bought rare coins at aggressive retail prices that built the company's profits into every transaction she'd thought was protecting her husband's legacy.

The forty-five thousand dollar gap between what she'd paid and what she'd get back wasn't fraud. There was no crime. The coins were real, the grades were accurate, the company had disclosed its prices. It was simply the cost of buying the wrong product from the wrong source without understanding the difference.

Barbara eventually sold most of her collection at a significant loss and started over with straightforward bullion. She was a wealth preserver who'd been sold a collector's product by people who understood her motivation well enough to pitch to it — but not well enough to actually serve it.

She didn't make that mistake twice. Neither will you.

This chapter is about making sure you don't make Barbara's mistake.

> *"I paid $80,000 for coins worth $35,000. The TV dealer said 'rare' and 'investment grade' but these trade at half what I paid. If only I'd read about numismatic premiums first."*

THE MOST IMPORTANT CONCEPT IN THIS CHAPTER

Everything in precious metals buying comes down to understanding one distinction: the difference between bullion and numismatic coins. Get this wrong and you can do everything else right and still lose significant money. Get it right and you have a filter that will protect you from the most common and most expensive mistakes in this market.

Bullion coins and bars are valued primarily for their precious metal content. When you buy a bullion product, you're paying for the gold or silver in it plus a modest premium that covers manufacturing, distribution, and dealer margin. When gold goes up ten percent, your bullion goes up approximately ten percent. When you want to sell, any coin dealer in the country will buy it from you at a price closely tied to the current spot price of the metal.

Numismatic coins are valued for their rarity, condition, historical significance, or collectability in addition to — and often far beyond — their metal content. A Morgan silver dollar that contains about three-quarters of an ounce of silver might sell for fifty dollars, five hundred dollars, or fifty thousand dollars depending on its date, mint mark, and grade. That enormous price range has nothing to do with silver's spot price and everything to do with what collectors are willing to pay for that specific coin.

The distinction matters enormously because these two products serve completely different purposes and require completely different knowledge to buy and sell intelligently. If your goal is wealth preservation or investment in precious metals as an asset class, you want bullion. Full stop. You're not trying to predict collector demand. You're trying to track metal prices, which is a much simpler and more transparent market.

Barbara's mistake was buying numismatic coins for wealth preservation purposes. She paid enormous premiums for collectability she didn't understand, couldn't evaluate, and ultimately couldn't sell at the prices she'd paid. The marketing that sold her those coins emphasized the grading and certification — which sounds like quality assurance — but grading and certification tell you a coin's condition, not whether you've paid a fair price for it.

> ***Here is a simple rule that will save you thousands of dollars: Unless you're genuinely interested in studying and collecting rare coins as a serious hobby, never buy anything with a significant numismatic premium. Stick with bullion. The simplicity is the point.***

GOLD VERSUS SILVER — UNDERSTANDING THE DIFFERENCE

The first practical decision most buyers face is whether to buy gold, silver, or some combination. There's no universal right answer — it depends on your buyer type, your budget, and what you're trying to accomplish.

Gold is wealth in concentrated form. At over four thousand dollars per ounce, a small physical amount represents substantial value. A handful of one-ounce gold coins in your jacket pocket is more wealth than most people keep in their savings account. Gold is the preferred metal for wealth preservation in large amounts because it's compact, universally recognized, and easy to transport and store. It also tends to be less volatile than silver over time.

Silver is more affordable and divisible but more bulky. At around sixty dollars per ounce, you need far more silver than gold to store the same dollar value — roughly sixty-seven times more by weight. But that divisibility is exactly what makes silver valuable for preppers and for smaller purchases. A one-ounce silver coin at sixty dollars is a useful transaction unit. A one-ounce gold coin at four thousand dollars is not.

Historically, silver has been more volatile than gold — it tends to amplify gold's moves in both directions, like a leveraged version of the same trade. When gold rises twenty percent, silver might rise forty percent. When gold falls fifteen percent, silver might fall thirty percent. For wealth preservers, that volatility is a reason to favor gold. For investors with conviction on precious metals, that leverage can be appealing — but only if you understand and can tolerate the swings.

For most people focused on wealth preservation, I recommend a mix weighted toward gold. Something like seventy percent gold and thirty percent silver gives you the stability of gold with some silver for divisibility. Adjust that ratio based on your budget — if you're working with a smaller amount, silver's lower entry price makes it more practical to start.

GOVERNMENT COINS VERSUS PRIVATE ROUNDS AND BARS

Within the bullion category, you have choices between government-minted coins, private mint rounds, and bars of various sizes. Each has advantages and trade-offs worth understanding.

Government-minted coins are produced by national mints — the US Mint, the Royal Canadian Mint, the South African Mint, and others. They carry the full faith and weight of national governments behind their stated purity and weight. They're the most universally recognized and trusted form of bullion worldwide. Walk into any coin shop in America with a Gold Eagle or a Silver Maple Leaf and you'll get a bid without hesitation.

Private rounds are produced by private mints and refiners. Companies like Sunshine Minting, APMEX's house brand, and dozens of others produce rounds and bars that meet the same purity standards as government coins at slightly lower premiums. The trade-off is slightly less universal recognition — some smaller dealers or private buyers might require testing on a private round they're less familiar with, while they'd accept a Gold Eagle on sight.

Bars come in various sizes from one ounce up to hundreds of ounces, produced by both government facilities and private refiners. Larger bars carry lower percentage premiums because the manufacturing cost is spread across more metal. A one-hundred-ounce silver bar carries a lower premium per ounce than ten separate one-ounce coins. The trade-off is liquidity — selling a hundred-ounce bar requires finding a buyer for the whole thing, while ten one-ounce coins can be sold individually as needed.

For most buyers, I recommend starting with government coins for your core gold holdings. American Gold Eagles, Canadian Gold Maple Leafs, and South African Krugerrands are the most liquid gold bullion products in the world. You will never struggle to sell them at fair prices. For silver, the premium difference between government coins and quality private rounds is often significant enough that a mix makes sense — government Eagles for maximum recognition, quality private rounds or bars when premium savings matter more.

> *"This chapter explains exactly what to avoid — rare coin premiums, TV dealer markups, numismatic traps. Knowledge saves thousands. I'll reference these notes before making any purchases."*

SPECIFIC PRODUCTS: WHAT I RECOMMEND

Let me be concrete about specific products worth knowing. For gold bullion, the workhorses are American Gold Eagles, Canadian Gold Maple Leafs, and South African Krugerrands.

American Gold Eagles are the most widely held and easily traded gold coins in America. They're twenty-two karat gold — ninety-one and two-thirds percent pure — alloyed with silver and copper for durability. They come in one-ounce, half-ounce, quarter-ounce, and tenth-ounce sizes. The one-ounce coin contains exactly one troy ounce of gold despite its slightly heavier total weight due to the alloy. Every coin dealer in America recognizes them instantly.

Canadian Gold Maple Leafs are twenty-four karat — ninety-nine point nine nine percent pure gold — and also come in multiple sizes. The purity makes them slightly more susceptible to surface marks than the hardier Eagles, but they're equally liquid and widely recognized internationally. Many buyers prefer them precisely because of the higher purity.

South African Krugerrands were the first modern one-ounce gold bullion coin, introduced in 1967, and they remain one of the most widely held gold coins worldwide. Like Eagles, they're twenty-two karat. They have no face value stamped on them — just their gold content — which makes them purely bullion instruments. Some buyers avoided them for political reasons during South Africa's apartheid era, but that history has no bearing on their value or liquidity today.

For silver bullion, American Silver Eagles are the American standard — one troy ounce of point nine nine nine fine silver, struck by the US Mint, with a legal tender face value of one dollar that has no relationship to their actual silver value. They command a higher premium than most silver alternatives, but their recognition and liquidity are unmatched. For someone who values instant, unquestioned acceptance above all, Silver Eagles are the answer.

Pre-1965 US silver coins — quarters, dimes, and half dollars containing ninety percent silver — are sold by dealers in bags or rolls measured by face value. A dollar's face value of pre-1965 coins contains approximately seventy-two hundredths of a troy ounce of silver. They're often called junk silver, which is a misleading name since they're genuinely valuable — they're just not numismatic. For preppers especially, these coins are ideal: instantly recognizable as real silver, priced accessibly, and available in small denominations.

FRACTIONAL COINS — WHEN SMALLER SIZES MAKE SENSE

Both gold and silver come in fractional sizes. Half-ounce, quarter-ounce, and tenth-ounce are common for gold. The advantage is lower absolute cost per purchase, making gold accessible when you can't afford a full one-ounce coin, and providing flexibility for partial liquidation when you don't want to sell a full ounce.

The disadvantage is higher premiums. A tenth-ounce Gold Eagle typically carries a premium twenty-five to thirty-five percent above spot compared to the three to five percent premium on a one-ounce coin. You're paying for the same manufacturing setup across less metal, which drives the per-ounce cost up significantly.

For most buyers, I recommend keeping the bulk of your holdings in one-ounce gold pieces for premium efficiency, but having some fractional pieces for flexibility. A few tenth-ounce or quarter-ounce coins give you options for partial sales or smaller transactions without forcing you to liquidate a full ounce when you need less.

WHAT TO AVOID — THE PRODUCT DANGER LIST

Now the part that will save the most money for the most people.

Avoid collectible or numismatic coins unless you're genuinely, seriously collecting as a hobby. We covered this with Barbara's story, but it deserves repeating because the marketing is aggressive and sophisticated. If a coin is described as 'rare,' 'limited edition,' 'investment grade,' 'certified,' 'graded,' or 'historically significant' in a sales context, those are signals that a premium beyond metal content is being charged. Sometimes that premium is legitimate for actual collectors. For wealth preservers and most investors, it is pure cost.

Avoid painted, colorized, or commemorative coins marketed as collectibles. These are frequently government bullion coins that have been modified by private companies and resold with enormous markups based on the modification. A Silver Eagle painted with a Christmas design or a Gold Eagle with a colored flag overlay is still just a Silver Eagle or Gold Eagle — the modification adds no value, and in some cases actually reduces the coin's appeal to serious buyers. The company charging you three times the coin's metal value for the artwork is the only one benefiting.

Avoid proof coins unless you're collecting for their beauty. Proof coins are specially made for collectors with mirror-like finishes and frosted design elements. They're genuinely beautiful objects. They also carry significant premiums over standard bullion strikes and are more susceptible to damage from handling — reducing their numismatic value if you touch them without cotton gloves. For wealth preservation, they're the wrong tool.

Be cautious with platinum and palladium unless you have specific reasons to want them. These are legitimate precious metals with real industrial applications, but their markets are smaller, more volatile, and more influenced by industrial demand than monetary factors. Unless you have a specific, informed thesis for owning them, the complexity isn't worth it for most buyers.

Avoid certificates, pool accounts, or paper gold products unless you understand exactly what you own. Some companies sell gold 'ownership' through certificates or allocated account programs rather than delivering physical metal. These products may or may not represent genuine allocated gold holdings. They require trusting the issuing company's integrity and financial stability. For most precious metals buyers — particularly those who want wealth outside the conventional financial system — physical metal in your own hands or secure storage is far preferable.

THE BULLION BUYER'S PRODUCT REFERENCE

1. Gold — First Choice: American Gold Eagle (1 oz). Twenty-two karat, maximum US recognition and liquidity, available in fractional sizes. The default recommendation for American buyers starting in gold.
2. Gold — Strong Alternatives: Canadian Gold Maple Leaf (24k, 99.99% pure), South African Krugerrand (22k, universally liquid), Austrian Gold Philharmonic, Australian Gold Kangaroo. All are government-minted, widely recognized, and excellent products.

3. Silver — First Choice: American Silver Eagle (1 oz, .999 fine). Highest recognition, highest premium. Worth paying for if you value instant, unquestioned acceptance.
4. Silver — Value Option: Pre-1965 US silver coins (90% silver quarters, dimes, half dollars). Sold by face value in bags or rolls. Ideal for preppers, practical for wealth preservers who want divisibility. Often called 'junk silver' — ignore the name.
5. Silver — Premium Savings: One-ounce rounds from reputable private mints (Sunshine Minting, APMEX, generic .999 rounds). Lower premiums than Silver Eagles, slightly less universal recognition. Good for bulk silver accumulation when cost efficiency matters.
6. Avoid: Numismatic and rare coins (unless you're a serious collector). Painted or colorized bullion. Proof coins for investment purposes. Pool accounts and certificates. Anything described as 'investment grade' or 'limited edition' by a television marketer.

A FINAL WORD ON PLATINUM AND PALLADIUM

I mentioned being cautious with platinum and palladium, but I should explain when they might make sense so you can make an informed decision rather than dismissing them entirely.

Both metals are used heavily in industrial applications — particularly in automotive catalytic converters — which creates demand patterns tied to car manufacturing cycles in ways that gold and silver are not. This makes their prices more susceptible to economic downturns that reduce auto production, and more sensitive to technological changes in the automotive industry.

Platinum historically traded above gold, but that relationship flipped in recent years and platinum is currently cheaper. Some buyers see this as an opportunity based on historical relationships reasserting themselves. That's a legitimate investment thesis — just make sure it's your thesis, based on your analysis, not something you were sold.

If you have substantial precious metals holdings and want to diversify within the metals space, adding some platinum or palladium can make sense. But for someone just beginning, or for anyone whose primary motivation is wealth preservation against currency and inflation risk, gold and silver are cleaner, more transparent, and more reliably liquid.

Master the fundamentals first. Complexity can come later, if it ever needs to come at all.

When you are ready to go deeper — into platinum group metals, futures markets, mining shares, assaying, and the full professional vocabulary of this industry — that is exactly what the **Precious Metals Trade Guide** covers. Two hundred and forty-four pages, over five hundred topics. Think of this Playbook as your foundation and the Trade Guide as the encyclopedia you reach for once the foundation is solid. More on that in the Conclusion.

★ ***I buy bullion, not stories. The metal is what holds the value — not the certificate, the grade, or the television pitch. Barbara learned this the hard way. I learned it here.*** ★

COMING UP NEXT

You know what to buy. Now you need to know where to buy it without getting ripped off.

Patricia lost seventeen thousand dollars to a professional-looking website that vanished completely. She did what seemed like reasonable research. She checked the site, read the testimonials, looked at the prices. In 2003, it was enough to fool her. Today the scams are more sophisticated, not less — and there are more of them.

Chapter Three will show you how to evaluate every type of precious metals seller, from local coin shops to online dealers to coin shows, and how to spot the red flags that legitimate operators never display.

CHAPTER THREE

WHERE TO BUY WITHOUT GETTING RIPPED OFF

> The seventeen thousand dollars Patricia sent to that online company looked like a smart purchase right up until the moment the website disappeared. Everything checked out — except the one thing that actually mattered.

In 2003, about six years after I'd relocated to Florida, I got a call from a woman named Patricia who'd found my name through a local business directory. She was crying, which doesn't happen often in this business, but when it does, it's usually bad.

She'd sent seventeen thousand dollars to an online company she'd found through a search engine. The website looked professional—clean design, reasonable prices, testimonials from satisfied customers, even a physical address listed in Nevada. She'd called and spoken with a sales representative who was friendly and knowledgeable. Everything seemed legitimate.

They'd promised delivery within two weeks. After three weeks with no metals and no response to her calls or emails, she started getting worried. After five weeks, she did some deeper research and discovered the company had dozens of complaints with the Better Business Bureau, a fake address, and a pattern of taking money and never delivering. The website disappeared a few days after her call to me. She never saw her seventeen thousand dollars or any gold.

Patricia wasn't careless or naive. She'd done what seemed like reasonable due diligence. The scammers had simply gotten good at looking legitimate. This was 2003, when internet commerce was less mature and the warning signs were harder to spot. Today the scams are even more sophisticated.

The question of where to buy precious metals is almost as important as the question of what to buy. You can make every right decision about products—buy the correct bullion at fair premiums with no numismatic markups—and still lose everything by buying from the wrong source. This chapter is about finding trustworthy places to buy and recognizing the red flags that signal trouble.

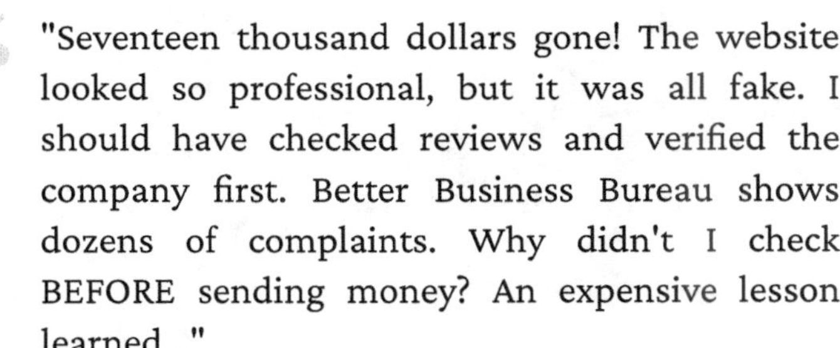

"Seventeen thousand dollars gone! The website looked so professional, but it was all fake. I should have checked reviews and verified the company first. Better Business Bureau shows dozens of complaints. Why didn't I check BEFORE sending money? An expensive lesson learned..."

LOCAL COIN SHOPS AND DEALERS

Let's start with the oldest and in many ways most straightforward option: local coin shops and precious metals dealers. These are brick-and-mortar businesses in your community where you can walk in, look at inventory, talk to someone face-to-face, and walk out with physical metal the same day.

The advantages of local dealers are substantial. You can inspect what you're buying before you hand over money. You can build a relationship with a dealer who gets to know you and your needs. You avoid shipping risks and insurance costs. You can often negotiate on price, especially for larger purchases. And if something goes wrong, you have a physical location and a person to deal with rather than trying to resolve problems with a distant company through email.

The challenge is finding a good local dealer and distinguishing them from bad ones. Not every coin shop is run by honest, knowledgeable people. Some are. Some aren't. Some charge fair prices. Some charge premiums that would make a used car salesman blush.

Here's how to evaluate a local dealer:

Check how long they've been in business. This isn't foolproof—some longtime dealers aren't great, and some newer dealers are excellent—but longevity suggests they've built a sustainable business rather than a quick-hit operation. A shop that's been operating in the same location for ten or twenty years is probably doing something right.

Watch how they price their products. Before you walk into any shop, check current spot prices for gold and silver online. You can find these on sites like Kitco.com or any precious metals dealer website. When you walk into the shop, compare their prices to spot. For bullion products like Gold Eagles or Silver Eagles, you should expect premiums of roughly five to ten percent for gold and ten to twenty percent for silver over spot, depending on market conditions and product availability. If they're charging thirty or forty percent premiums on standard bullion, walk out.

Pay attention to the spread between buy and sell prices. Ask what they're paying to buy back a Gold Eagle or Silver Eagle, and compare it to what they're selling the same coin for. A reasonable spread might be six to ten percent. If they're buying at sixty percent of spot and selling at one-forty percent of spot, they're operating on margins that should make you suspicious.

Ask questions and evaluate their knowledge. A good dealer should be able to explain products, discuss market conditions, and answer questions without high-pressure sales tactics. They should be willing to educate you rather than just push you toward their highest-margin products. If someone is aggressively steering you toward expensive numismatic coins when you've expressed interest in bullion, that's a red flag.

Look for membership in professional organizations. Membership in the Professional Numismatists Guild (PNG) or similar organizations isn't a guarantee, but it suggests the dealer has made commitments to ethical business practices and has enough standing in the industry to be accepted.

Check online reviews, but take them with salt. Look at Google reviews, Better Business Bureau ratings, and industry-specific forums. A dealer with hundreds of positive reviews over years is probably legitimate. But also recognize that reviews can be manipulated. Look for patterns in complaints rather than isolated incidents.

Trust your instincts. If something feels off—if the sales pitch is too aggressive, if the prices seem too good to be true, if the dealer seems more interested in selling you expensive products than understanding your needs—walk away. There are other dealers.

I ran my shop in Woodstock, Illinois for ten years, and my goal was always to build long-term relationships rather than maximize profit on every transaction. I'd rather make a fair margin on someone's first purchase and have them come back for twenty years than squeeze them once and never see them again. Good dealers think this way. Bad dealers think about today's commission.

ONLINE DEALERS: THE CONVENIENCE TRADE-OFF

Online precious metals dealers have grown enormously over the past two decades. Companies like APMEX, Money Metals, SD Bullion, and others ship millions of dollars in precious metals every week. They offer convenience, selection, competitive pricing, and the ability to compare options from your computer.

The advantages are obvious. You can shop from home, compare prices across multiple dealers instantly, and often find better selection than local shops can stock. Major online dealers handle such large volume that they often have lower premiums than small local shops. And reputable online dealers are just as legitimate as good local shops—they're just operating through a different business model.

The disadvantages are that you can't inspect products before buying, you have to trust shipping and insurance, you're dealing with companies at a distance, and if problems arise, resolution is more complicated than walking back into a shop.

Here's how to evaluate online dealers:

Stick with established, well-known companies. APMEX (American Precious Metals Exchange) has been operating since 2000 and is one of the largest dealers in the country. Money Metals, SD Bullion, Provident Metals, and a handful of others have built strong reputations over years or decades. These companies have too much to lose to scam customers. They're not perfect—nobody is—but they're vastly safer than unknown companies with six-month-old websites.

Check their Better Business Bureau rating and look at complaint patterns. Every large dealer will have some complaints—it's inevitable with thousands of transactions. What matters is how they respond to complaints and whether there are patterns suggesting systemic problems. A company with an A+ rating that responds to and resolves most complaints is probably fine. A company with dozens of unresolved complaints about not delivering products or charging hidden fees should be avoided.

Verify they have secure payment processing and proper website security. Look for "https" in the web address and a lock icon in your browser. Legitimate dealers use secure payment processing that protects your financial information. If a website is asking you to wire money to foreign accounts or pay with untraceable methods, run away.

Understand their shipping, insurance, and return policies before you order. How long does shipping take? Is insurance included? What happens if products are lost or damaged in transit? What's their return policy if you're not satisfied? These should all be clearly explained on their website. If they're not, or if the policies seem unreasonable, consider shopping elsewhere.

Be aware of price volatility. Precious metals prices change constantly. Some online dealers lock in your price the moment you place an order. Others hold orders for "verification" and then claim prices changed before they could ship, sticking you with higher prices. Reputable dealers lock prices immediately.

Start with a small order if you're trying a new dealer. Even with established companies, your first order should be modest until you've verified they deliver as promised and the products meet your expectations. Once you're confident, you can place larger orders.

Patricia's story from the beginning of this chapter happened because she didn't stick with established dealers. She found a company that looked legitimate but had no track record and no verifiable history. Today, with more mature online reviews and better information availability, it's easier to avoid such scams —but they still exist. The simple rule is: if you haven't heard of the company, if they don't have extensive, verifiable reviews spanning years, shop elsewhere.

COIN SHOWS: OPPORTUNITIES FOR THE PREPARED

Coin and precious metals shows happen regularly in most regions—monthly in major cities, a few times a year in smaller markets. These are events where dozens or hundreds of dealers set up tables in convention centers or hotel ballrooms to sell coins, bullion, and collectibles directly to the public.

For knowledgeable buyers, coin shows can be excellent opportunities. You can compare prices from many dealers in one place. You can find products that aren't readily available elsewhere. You can often negotiate better prices than you'd get in a shop, especially toward the end of a show when dealers want to move inventory rather than pack it up. And you can build relationships with dealers from around the region or country.

For unprepared buyers, coin shows can be dangerous. You're dealing with dozens of unfamiliar dealers in a crowded, stimulating environment. Some dealers at shows are excellent professionals. Others are marginal operators who show up to move questionable inventory they can't sell through regular channels. Without knowledge and preparation, it's easy to make expensive mistakes.

If you're going to buy at coin shows, here's how to do it safely:

Know prices before you arrive. Check spot prices and typical premiums for the products you're interested in. Write them down or keep them on your phone. This prevents you from getting caught up in the excitement and paying far more than you should.

Bring testing equipment. At minimum, bring a strong neodymium magnet (gold and silver aren't magnetic, but many fakes are) and a digital jeweler's scale if you have one. For anyone serious about buying at shows or from private sellers, I strongly recommend investing in a Sigma Metalytics Precious Metal Verifier or similar electronic tester—these devices can verify authenticity without damaging the coin and are worth every penny if you're making purchases of a few thousand dollars or more.

That said, reputable dealers at coin shows will have their own testing equipment and should be willing to demonstrate authenticity right in front of you using their Sigma tester, XRF analyzer, or other professional devices. If a dealer refuses to test products or gets defensive when you ask to verify, walk away immediately. Good dealers welcome verification because it builds trust.

Don't buy expensive items from dealers you can't verify. If you're spending hundreds or thousands of dollars, make sure you know who you're buying from. Get their business card. Check if they have an established shop or online presence. Don't hand cash to someone you can't track down later if problems arise.

Be especially cautious of "too good to be true" deals. If everyone else at the show is selling Gold Eagles at spot plus five percent, and one dealer is selling them at spot plus one percent, ask yourself why. Maybe he's moving inventory at cost to generate cash flow. Maybe he's got fakes. Probably the latter.

Take your time and don't feel pressured. Good dealers at shows are happy to answer questions and let you think. Dealers who pressure you to buy immediately or who get defensive about testing products are dealers to avoid.

I've attended and sold at hundreds of coin shows over the decades, from small local events to major national conventions. The best shows, like the ones sponsored by PNG, require dealers to meet certain standards. Smaller, unregulated shows can be more variable. If you're new to this, stick with larger, established shows until you develop judgment about dealers and products.

BANKS: A LIMITED BUT SAFE OPTION

Some people don't realize that banks occasionally sell precious metals. Not all banks, and not as a major part of their business, but some do. If your bank offers precious metals, this can be a very safe option, though usually not the most economical.

Banks that sell metals are typically offering products from reputable mints at fair premiums. You won't get the absolute best prices—banks aren't competing on premium efficiency—but you also have essentially zero risk of fraud or counterfeit products. And you can buy with familiar banking relationships and payment methods.

The downsides are limited selection and typically higher premiums than specialized dealers. Banks usually offer only the most basic products—American Gold Eagles, maybe some silver products—and they're not going to negotiate on price or provide the kind of personalized service a good coin shop offers.

If you value the safety and convenience of buying through your bank over getting the absolute best price, and if your bank offers precious metals, it's a legitimate option. Just check their premiums against other sources to make sure you're not overpaying significantly.

ESTATE SALES AND PRIVATE SALES: HIGH RISK, HIGH REWARD

Occasionally you'll encounter opportunities to buy precious metals through estate sales, private sellers, or similar non-dealer sources. Someone inherited coins they want to sell. A family is liquidating a collection. Someone has gold jewelry they're selling for scrap value.

These situations can offer excellent opportunities if you know what you're doing. You might buy at below retail prices or find interesting pieces at good values. But they also carry substantial risks.

The biggest risk is authenticity. When you buy from a dealer, you have some recourse if products turn out to be fake. When you buy from a private party at an estate sale, you're on your own. If you don't know how to test and verify what you're buying, you can lose everything.

The second risk is legal. Make sure you're buying from someone who has the legal right to sell. Buying stolen property, even unknowingly, can create serious problems.

The third risk is simply overpaying. Just because someone is selling privately doesn't mean they're offering below-market prices. Many private sellers have inflated ideas of what their items are worth.

If you're going to buy from private sources:

Test everything thoroughly before you exchange money. Bring testing equipment. Take your time. Don't let anyone pressure you.

Get identification and a bill of sale. You want documentation of who you bought from, what you bought, and for how much.

Be prepared to walk away from anything questionable. There are plenty of legitimate sources for precious metals. You don't need to take risks on private deals unless the opportunity is clearly legitimate and clearly advantageous.

Consider using a dealer as an intermediary. Some dealers will verify and authenticate items from estate sales or private collections for a fee. If you're looking at a significant purchase from a private source, paying a dealer fifty or a hundred dollars to verify authenticity can save you thousands.

I've made excellent buys at estate sales over the years, but I've also walked away from dozens of situations that looked questionable. The deals that look too good to be true usually are.

WHAT TO AVOID COMPLETELY

Let's talk about sources you should never buy from, regardless of how good the opportunity seems.

Never buy from door-to-door sellers or unsolicited contacts. If someone shows up at your house or approaches you randomly offering to sell precious metals, it's a scam. Legitimate dealers don't operate this way.

Never wire money to foreign accounts or use untraceable payment methods for dealers you don't know. If someone wants you to wire money to Nigeria or Malaysia or anywhere else foreign, or if they want payment in gift cards or cryptocurrency, you're being scammed.

Never buy from social media ads or pop-up websites with no track record. Facebook ads and similar platforms are full of precious metals scams. New websites appear, look professional, take orders and money, and disappear. Stick with established dealers.

Be extremely cautious with classified ads and online marketplaces. Craigslist, Facebook Marketplace, and similar platforms can work for local in-person transactions if you're knowledgeable and careful, but they're also full of scammers and people selling fakes. If you buy through these channels, meet in public places, bring testing equipment, and don't carry large amounts of cash unless you're certain of what you're getting.

Avoid high-pressure television and radio marketers. Companies that advertise aggressively on TV and radio often charge enormous premiums and push customers toward expensive numismatic products using fear-based marketing. There are legitimate dealers who advertise, but be extremely cautious and compare their prices carefully against other sources.

THE DEALER VETTING CHECKLIST — BEFORE YOU SEND MONEY

1. **Check how long they've been in business.** Search for the company name plus "founded" or "established." Look for at least five years of verifiable history. New companies aren't automatically bad, but they carry more risk.
2. **Verify their Better Business Bureau rating and complaint history.** Go to BBB.org and search for the dealer. Look at their rating, but more importantly, read the complaints. Are they responding? Are they resolving issues? Are there patterns that suggest systemic problems?
3. **Search for reviews across multiple platforms.** Google reviews, Trustpilot, Reddit, and precious metals forums. Look for hundreds of reviews spanning years, not dozens of five-star reviews all posted in the same month. Read the negative reviews carefully—do they describe experiences that would concern you?
4. **Verify their physical location if they claim to have one.** Use Google Maps Street View to confirm the address exists and looks like a real business location. Call the number and talk to a real person. Ask questions about their inventory and policies.
5. **Compare their pricing to at least two other established dealers.** If their premiums are significantly lower than everyone else, ask yourself why. Occasionally you find an exceptional deal. More

often you find a scam or a dealer pushing counterfeit products.

6. **Check their shipping and insurance policies in detail.** Are shipments insured? What happens if products are lost or damaged? What's their return policy? These should be clearly explained on their website. If they're not, or if you have to dig to find them, that's a red flag.
7. **Test their customer service before you buy.** Call or email with a question. How responsive are they? How knowledgeable? Do they pressure you toward expensive products or help you understand options? Their behavior before the sale predicts their behavior after.

The time to vet a dealer is before you send money. Once the money is gone, your leverage is gone. Do the homework up front.

YOUR NEXT STEP

Before you buy anything, identify at least two or three sources you can use and verify they're legitimate. If you have good local dealers, visit them, compare prices, and see who you're comfortable with. If you're planning to buy online, make a list of the major dealers, check their reviews and reputation, and bookmark their websites for price comparison.

Don't buy from the first place you find or from whoever happens to have the best marketing. Take time to verify legitimacy, compare prices, and build relationships with sources you trust.

The right dealer will educate you, offer fair prices, and treat you as a long-term customer rather than a one-time commission. The wrong dealer will pressure you, charge excessive premiums, and make you question the whole idea of buying precious metals.

Find the right sources first. Then you can buy with confidence.

★ I verify dealer reputation thoroughly using BBB ratings, customer reviews, and personal research before I send money to anyone. Seventeen minutes of homework can save seventeen thousand dollars of loss. ★

COMING UP NEXT

The fake Krugerrand's I almost bought in 1993 weighed perfectly, measured perfectly, and looked exactly right. They passed every test I'd relied on for thirty years—until one didn't.

Seven authentication methods. Which fakes each one catches. Which ones tungsten defeats. And the exact testing sequence that turns a nervous purchase into a confident one. Chapter Five might save you more money than any other chapter in this book.

CHAPTER FOUR

PRICING SECRETS: PREMIUMS & SPREADS

> *The number on the price tag is not the number that matters. Understanding what you actually pay — and what you'll actually receive — is the most valuable financial skill in this market.*

Most people think buying precious metals is straightforward. Check the gold price. Find a dealer. Pay that price plus a small fee. Done.

Then they try to sell a year later and discover they need prices to have risen five, seven, ten percent just to break even. The gold did exactly what they expected. The numbers still don't work. And nobody warned them.

This is the most common form of financial disappointment in the precious metals market, and it has nothing to do with fraud or bad products. It happens to intelligent, informed buyers who simply didn't understand the true cost of their transactions going in.

The problem has a name: the round-trip cost. It's the combined effect of the premium you pay when you buy and the discount you accept when you sell. It's the real number — the one that determines whether precious metals are working for you or against you. And almost nobody explains it clearly before you buy.

This chapter does. By the time you finish it, you'll be able to calculate the true cost of any precious metals transaction in about three minutes, compare dealers on the number that actually matters, and make intelligent purchase decisions that account for reality rather than the price you see advertised.

START HERE: UNDERSTANDING SPOT PRICE

Everything in precious metals pricing begins with a single number called the spot price. This is the current market price for immediate delivery of one troy ounce of metal — the price at which large institutional players are trading gold or silver right now, in bulk, on global exchanges. Note: all specific dollar figures used in this chapter are illustrative examples only, based on prices shown in the accompanying images. Gold and silver prices change constantly — always check Kitco.com or a major dealer's website for today's actual spot price before making any calculations.

Spot prices are set in continuous global markets and move constantly throughout every trading day. You can check them in real time on sites like Kitco.com, the APMEX website, or any major financial platform. When the news says gold is at four thousand dollars, they're quoting spot price.

Here is the single most important thing to understand about spot price: you will never buy physical precious metals at spot price. And you will never sell physical precious metals at spot price. The spot price is the foundation everything else is built on — but it is not the price you will pay or receive.

The gap between spot price and your actual transaction price is where the entire economics of precious metals trading live. Understanding that gap — what creates it, what's reasonable, and how to minimize it — is what this chapter is about.

> *"Understanding the base price first — then I can spot if a dealer is charging fair premiums or trying to rip me off. Checking three different price sources to make sure I have accurate information. Knowledge is power."*

THE PREMIUM: WHAT YOU PAY ABOVE SPOT

The premium is the amount above spot price that you pay when buying precious metals. Look at the image on the previous page — you can see spot gold shown at $4,200 per ounce on the Kitco app. If a dealer sells you a Gold Eagle for $4,325 at that spot price, the premium is $125 — about three percent. That same percentage calculation applies whatever today's actual spot happens to be.

Premiums exist for entirely legitimate reasons. Someone refined the raw metal to high purity, which requires sophisticated equipment and energy. Someone designed the coin, manufactured the dies, struck it under high pressure, inspected it, packaged it, and shipped it. Someone warehoused it. Someone marketed it to you and processed your transaction. All of that has real cost.

The question is never whether premiums should exist — they absolutely must. The question is how much premium is reasonable, and when you're being charged more than the market fairly requires.

For standard one-ounce gold bullion coins — Gold Eagles, Maple Leafs, Krugerrands — reasonable premiums from established dealers typically run three to six percent above spot in normal market conditions. Below three percent is exceptional value. Above eight percent starts raising eyebrows. Above ten percent requires a very good explanation.

Silver premiums tend to be higher in percentage terms. American Silver Eagles typically carry premiums of twelve to twenty percent or more above spot, because the manufacturing cost is large relative to the metal value. Generic one-ounce silver rounds from private mints carry lower premiums — often eight to fourteen percent — because you're not paying for the government mint's overhead or the Eagle's legal tender status.

Premium percentages also vary by product size. A tenth-ounce Gold Eagle might carry a premium of twenty-five to thirty-five percent because the same manufacturing cost is spread across one-tenth the metal. A one-hundred-ounce silver bar might carry only three to five percent because the manufacturing cost per ounce is minimal at scale.

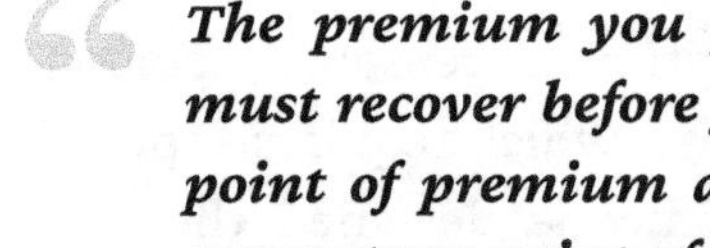

> ***The premium you pay going in is a cost you must recover before you profit. Every percentage point of premium above the market norm is a percentage point of price appreciation you need just to break even. Knowing what's reasonable — and shopping until you find it — is not optional. It is the job.***

THE SPREAD: THE NUMBER NOBODY TELLS YOU ABOUT

Here is where most buyers get their first unpleasant surprise. The spread is the difference between what a dealer charges to sell metal and what that same dealer will pay to buy it back. And it is almost always larger than you expect.

Let's make this concrete using the spot price shown in the images in this chapter — $4,200 per ounce. A dealer sells you a Gold Eagle at $4,325 — a premium of $125, or three percent above spot. Reasonable.

Now you want to sell that same coin back six months later. The spot price hasn't moved. You call the dealer expecting something close to what you paid. They quote you four thousand one hundred and fifty dollars — fifty dollars below spot.

You paid one hundred twenty-five dollars above spot. You received fifty dollars below spot. Your round-trip cost on a four thousand dollar coin is one hundred seventy-five dollars — more than four percent — before gold moved a single dollar in either direction.

That round-trip cost is the number that actually determines whether precious metals make financial sense for your situation and timeline. A wealth preserver planning to hold for twenty years barely notices it. An investor planning to sell within eighteen months needs gold to rise meaningfully just to recover it. An investor planning to sell within six months is almost certainly in a losing position from day one.

This is not the dealer's fault. Spreads exist because dealers need margin both coming and going. When they buy your coin, they carry it in inventory until they find a buyer, absorbing market risk the entire time. Tight, efficient operations run tight spreads. High-overhead, high-marketing operations run wide spreads. The variance between dealers on this single number can be dramatic.

> *"Gold at $4,200/oz — now I understand how premiums work. That dealer wanting $4,600 for a Gold Eagle is charging 9.5% premium. Spot price plus a reasonable premium equals a fair price. No more getting ripped off by fancy sales pitches."*

A REAL TRANSACTION: BREAKING DOWN THE NUMBERS

Let's walk through a concrete comparison so you can see exactly how this plays out. We'll look at three dealers selling the same one-ounce Gold Eagle on the same day, when spot gold is four thousand two hundred dollars.

DEALER COMPARISON — ILLUSTRATIVE EXAMPLE USING IMAGE SPOT PRICE OF $4,200/OZ

Dealer A — The Tight Operator

Sell price (what you pay): $4,325 (+$125 above spot, 3.0% premium)

Buy price (what they pay you): $4,150 (-$50 below spot, 1.2% discount)

Round-trip cost: $175 (4.2% of spot) — Profitable with modest gold appreciation

Dealer B — The Expensive Option

Sell price (what you pay): $4,515 (+$315 above spot, 7.5% premium)

Buy price (what they pay you): $3,990 (-$210 below spot, 5.0% discount)

Round-trip cost: $525 (12.5% of spot) — Gold must rise over 12% before you profit

Dealer C — The High-Markup Problem

Sell price (what you pay): $4,830 (+$630 above spot, 15% premium)

Buy price (what they pay you): $3,780 (-$420 below spot, 10% discount)

Round-trip cost: $1,050 (25% of spot) — You are in a deep hole from day one

Now scale those numbers up to a ten-ounce purchase — roughly $42,000 at the $4,200 spot shown in these images. Dealer A costs you $1,750 in round-trip transaction costs. Dealer B costs you $5,250. Dealer C costs you $10,500. At today's actual spot price your absolute dollar figures will differ, but the percentage relationships — and the lesson — remain identical.

That is an eight thousand seven hundred and fifty dollar difference between the best and worst dealer on this list — purely on transaction costs, before gold moves a single dollar. This is why comparing premiums and spreads across multiple dealers before you buy is not optional diligence. It is the single highest-return activity available to a precious metals buyer.

And notice what Dealer C looks like. Fifteen percent premium on the way in. Ten percent discount on the way out. Those are the numbers produced by aggressive television marketers and high-overhead operations that spend enormous money on advertising, celebrity endorsements, and slick fulfillment. The coin is real. The gold is genuine. The price is a disaster.

> *"This dealer's 'low premium' doesn't help if their buyback price is terrible. Round-trip cost is what really matters. Shopping around will save me hundreds per purchase — thousands over time. Worth the extra hour of research."*

PREMIUM PATTERNS BY PRODUCT TYPE

Understanding typical premium ranges for different products helps you spot outliers immediately. When a dealer quotes you something dramatically outside these ranges, you know to ask why.

Government bullion coins — Gold Eagles, Maple Leafs, Krugerrands — typically carry three to six percent gold premiums and twelve to twenty percent silver premiums in normal market conditions. These are the benchmark products. If a dealer is significantly above these ranges on standard coins, they're telling you something about their business model.

Private mint rounds and bars typically carry lower premiums — two to five percent for gold and eight to fourteen percent for silver. You're not paying for government mint overhead, legal tender status, or the recognition premium that comes with a widely known product. The trade-off is slightly less universal liquidity, which matters more in some situations than others.

Pre-1965 US silver coins — what dealers call junk silver — typically trade close to their silver melt value with a modest premium of five to ten percent. These coins trade on silver content, not collectability, which keeps pricing transparent and relatively tight.

Large bars carry the lowest premiums because the manufacturing cost per ounce is minimal at scale. A one-hundred-ounce silver bar might carry only two to four percent premium. The trade-off is the liquidity constraint of needing to sell the whole thing at once.

Fractional coins carry the highest percentage premiums because the same manufacturing cost is spread across less metal. A tenth-ounce Gold Eagle at a twenty-five percent premium is normal and expected — not a rip-off, just the economics of small denomination manufacturing.

WHEN PREMIUMS SPIKE: SUPPLY AND DEMAND

One thing that consistently surprises new buyers is how much premiums can vary over time. You might research Silver Eagles and find typical premiums of fifteen percent, then try to buy during a market panic and find every dealer charging twenty-five to thirty percent — or simply out of stock entirely.

This happened dramatically in March 2020 when COVID sent markets into chaos. Spot gold actually dropped initially — institutional players were selling everything liquid to cover margin calls elsewhere. But physical precious metals premiums exploded upward because retail demand surged while mint production and dealer supply chains were disrupted. People who needed to check a mental health box about owning gold in a crisis found that the premiums had eaten most of the benefit of any price increase.

If you're trying to buy during a premium spike, your options are limited. Waiting is the most rational response if your situation allows it — premium spikes are temporary, and supply typically catches up with demand within weeks or months. Shopping aggressively across multiple dealers matters more during spikes than at any other time, because the variance between dealers widens. And considering alternative products — Krugerrands when Eagles are scarce, generic rounds when Silver Eagles carry huge premiums — can capture the metal exposure you want at more reasonable cost.

The deeper lesson is that buying during calm markets — when nobody is talking about precious metals and premiums are tight — is almost always better than buying during the crisis moments that make people suddenly want gold. Dollar cost averaging, which we'll cover in Chapter Seven, is the practical response to this reality.

NEGOTIATING: WHEN IT WORKS AND WHEN IT DOESN'T

People often ask whether precious metals prices are negotiable. The honest answer is sometimes, in specific situations, with specific types of dealers — and never in ways that overcome fundamentally uncompetitive pricing.

Online dealers with published prices don't negotiate. Their margins are thin, their pricing is competitive by design, and they're processing thousands of transactions. There's nothing to negotiate and no mechanism to do it. What you see is what you pay.

Local shops sometimes negotiate, especially on larger purchases. If you're buying ten thousand dollars worth of gold in a single transaction, it's entirely reasonable to ask about volume pricing. Many dealers will shave a few dollars per coin for significant orders — not because they're doing you a favor, but because a certain volume at a modest discount is better business than losing the sale entirely.

Estate and private sales offer the most negotiating room, because pricing is subjective and sellers are often motivated. But negotiating a private sale down to a reasonable price requires knowing what reasonable is — which circles back to everything in this chapter.

What never works is trying to negotiate on the basis of ignorance or wishful thinking. Asking a dealer to sell you a Gold Eagle at spot price is not negotiating — it's demonstrating that you don't understand the market. The better approach is always to shop the market until you find a dealer whose base prices are already fair, rather than trying to beat bad prices down to good ones.

THE PRICING HOMEWORK — BEFORE YOU BUY ANYTHING

1. Check spot price right now. Go to Kitco.com or any major dealer's website and note the current spot price for gold and silver. Write it down with the time. This is your baseline — every price you're quoted today is a deviation from this number, and the size and direction of that deviation tells you what a dealer's business model actually is.
2. Get quotes from at least three dealers for the specific product you want to buy. Calculate the premium percentage for each: (dealer price minus spot) divided by spot, multiplied by one hundred. Write each one down. You are building a comparison, not making a decision yet.
3. Ask each dealer their current buyback price for the same product. Do not accept 'it depends on the market' — ask for today's number at today's spot. Calculate round-trip cost: sell price minus buyback price. This is the number that actually matters. Compare it across dealers.
4. Factor your holding period into the math. If Dealer A has a round-trip cost of four percent and Dealer B has eight percent, and you plan to hold for ten years, the difference is meaningful but not dramatic. If you plan to hold for eighteen months, Dealer B may require gold to appreciate considerably before you see a profit. The same premium calculation means very different things for different timeframes.

5. Check current premium ranges against the typical benchmarks in this chapter. One-ounce gold coins at three to six percent. Silver Eagles at twelve to twenty percent. Generic silver rounds at eight to fourteen percent. Any quote significantly above these ranges for standard products requires an explanation. If a dealer can't give you one, they have given you their answer.

THE ONE NUMBER TO REMEMBER

If you take nothing else from this chapter, take this: always ask for the buyback price before you commit to buying. Always.

Not after you've decided. Not as a courtesy after the transaction is complete. Before. As part of your evaluation of whether this is the right dealer for this purchase.

Any legitimate dealer will give you a buyback quote immediately and without hesitation. It's a standard question that real buyers ask, and experienced dealers expect it. A dealer who deflects, hedges, becomes evasive, or makes you feel awkward for asking has answered your question more honestly than anything they might say directly.

The round-trip cost is your money. You have an absolute right to know it before you commit to a transaction. Never let anyone make you feel otherwise.

★ ***I know my round-trip cost before I commit to any purchase. The premium going in and the spread coming out are both my money — and I calculate them both before anyone gets any of it.*** ★

COMING UP NEXT

The tungsten Krugerrands that open Chapter Five weighed correctly, measured correctly, and looked exactly right. They passed every test except one — the test the dealer almost didn't run.

Seven authentication methods. Which fakes each one catches. Which ones tungsten defeats. And the exact testing sequence that turns a nervous purchase into a confident one. Chapter Five has saved more of my customers' money than any other chapter in this book.

CHAPTER FIVE

HOW TO VERIFY YOU'RE GETTING REAL METAL

> *Buying from the right dealer at the right price means nothing if what arrives isn't what you paid for. Authentication is not paranoia — it is the final step that makes everything else worthwhile.*

Tuesday afternoon, 1993. A man walked into my Florida shop — expensive suit, leather briefcase, easy confidence. He had twenty Krugerrand's and a story about a real estate deal closing Thursday. He needed quick cash and was willing to sell fifty dollars below spot on each coin. I had my checkbook out before he finished the sentence. Then something made me stop. The way he kept checking his watch. The way he was already calculating his exit. I told him I wanted to run the electronic probe before we talked numbers. He stiffened — just slightly — but I saw it. I insisted. He relented. I touched the probe to the third coin and the detector screamed. Tungsten. Twenty-five dollars' worth of tungsten core wrapped in a microscopic shell of real gold, machined to exact weight and dimensions, stamped with a convincing die. He was out the door before I said another word. I heard later he'd already taken two other shops for the same coins. Both of them bought without testing. I've thought about those Krugerrands many times in the thirty years since. Not just because of how close I came to losing fifty thousand dollars — though that's sobering enough — but because of how good they were.

> *"These look absolutely perfect — weight, dimensions, color all correct. But something made me test them anyway. TUNGSTEN. The tester is screaming. Nearly lost $50,000 to sophisticated fakes. Always verify — even after 30 years."*

Those coins had passed every physical test available to me — weight, dimensions, color, magnetism. The luster, the fine detail on the springbok and Paul Kruger's profile, all of it convincing under careful visual examination. Every test I might have run without an electronic probe would have cleared them.

The counterfeiter who made them understood something important: a fake only needs to beat the tests its buyer actually runs. Build it to pass visual inspection and you beat most buyers. Build it to pass the magnet and the scale and you beat almost everyone. A well-made tungsten core wrapped in a precise gold shell will pass every test except electromagnetic conductivity — and most buyers never run that one.

That's the arms race at the heart of precious metals authentication. Counterfeits have become sophisticated because the rewards justify sophisticated investment. And the market for physical precious metals has grown large enough to make that investment very worthwhile for the people willing to operate that way.

But here's the other side of that equation: authentication methods have kept pace. The same technology that lets bad actors create better fakes has produced better detection equipment, at lower prices, accessible to individual buyers. The tests available to you today would have seemed extraordinary to me when I was starting in this business.

This chapter walks you through every meaningful authentication method, from what you can do with twenty dollars' worth of equipment to what professional dealers use on high-value transactions. By the end, you'll know exactly what you need for the way you buy — and you'll understand why the most important authentication habit costs nothing at all.

> ***A fake only needs to beat the tests its buyer actually runs. Which means the single most protective thing you can do is simply decide — firmly, in advance, before any transaction — that you will always run every test you have available. Not most of the time. Every time. Without exception.***

WHY COUNTERFEITS EXIST AND WHERE THEY COME FROM

Before diving into detection, it helps to understand what you're actually defending against. This isn't about being paranoid — it's about being realistic.

The economics of counterfeiting precious metals are straightforward and brutal. If you can produce something that costs twenty-five dollars in materials and sell it as a product worth over a thousand dollars, your margin is extraordinary. That margin justifies real investment — proper equipment, skilled labour, quality control, and sophisticated distribution. The most dangerous counterfeits don't come from individuals working in garages. They come from organized operations with genuine engineering capability.

Most sophisticated counterfeits originate overseas, primarily in China, where manufacturing infrastructure and precious metals expertise intersect with insufficient enforcement. They enter the market through multiple channels — online sales, coin shows, private sellers who may not even know what they're holding, and occasionally dealers who've been deceived themselves.

The most dangerous fakes are tungsten-core coins and bars. Tungsten has nearly the same density as gold — nineteen point three grams per cubic centimeter versus nineteen point three for gold — which means a tungsten core machined to exact dimensions and plated with real gold will match weight and size specifications almost perfectly. A well-made tungsten fake will pass visual inspection, magnet test, weight verification, and dimension checking. It requires electromagnetic or X-ray testing to detect.

Silver fakes tend to be less sophisticated because silver's lower value makes elaborate counterfeiting less profitable. Most silver fakes are either obvious base metal plated items or lower-quality products that fail basic testing. The exception is high-value silver — large bars and premium products — where the economics justify more sophisticated fakery.

The good news is that counterfeits disproportionately target the most common, highest-value products from the most recognizable government mints. Generic rounds from smaller private mints are rarely counterfeited because the volume isn't there. Buying primarily from established dealers dramatically reduces your encounter probability. But it doesn't reduce it to zero, which is why you test anyway.

THE SEVEN TESTS — FROM SIMPLEST TO MOST DEFINITIVE

Here are the authentication methods available to you, organized from the simplest and cheapest to the most thorough and expensive. Most buyers need the first three or four. Serious buyers who purchase regularly from varied sources should consider the fifth and sixth. Understanding all seven helps you make intelligent decisions about where to invest in your own capability.

- **TEST 1: VISUAL INSPECTION**

Test: #1 — Visual Inspection

Difficulty: Beginner — no equipment required

Equipment Cost: Free

Catches: Obvious fakes, poor strikes, wrong color, packaging tampering

Limitation: Cannot catch well-made fakes — good counterfeits look genuinely good

---

The first line of defense is looking carefully at what you're buying, with knowledge of what genuine coins look like. This isn't foolproof — good fakes look good — but it catches obvious problems and costs nothing.

Check the strike quality. Genuine government coins are produced with precision dies under enormous pressure. Design details should be crisp and complete — sharp edges on lettering, clean relief on design elements, consistent finish across the field. Soft, mushy, or incomplete details suggest inferior manufacturing.

Examine the color and luster. Real gold has a distinctive warm color and a particular way of reflecting light that's genuinely difficult to replicate perfectly in base metal plating. Hold it under good light and compare it to a known genuine coin if you have one. Your eye will develop over time — every coin you handle teaches you something.

Check packaging where applicable. Many bullion products come in sealed capsules or original mint packaging with security features. Tampered packaging isn't proof of a fake, but it's a flag worth noting. Genuine products from reputable dealers typically arrive in original, undamaged condition.

- **TEST 2: THE MAGNET TEST**

Test: #2 — The Magnet Test

Difficulty: Beginner — takes thirty seconds

Equipment Cost: Under $10 for a strong neodymium magnet

Catches: Magnetic metals — steel, iron, nickel-core fakes

Limitation: Doesn't catch non-magnetic fakes — tungsten, copper, brass all pass this test

---

Gold and silver are not magnetic. Hold a strong neodymium magnet near genuine precious metal and there should be no attraction whatsoever. This test is instant, non-destructive, and catches certain categories of cheap fakes.

The critical caveat: this test only catches magnetic metals. Tungsten — the most dangerous counterfeit core material — is not magnetic and will pass this test easily. Copper and brass also pass. A tungsten-core coin will sail through a magnet test without a flicker.

Use a strong neodymium magnet, not a weak refrigerator magnet. The stronger the magnet, the more sensitive the test. You can buy adequate neodymium magnets online for a few dollars. Run this test on every piece you buy because it's instant and catches some fakes at zero cost — just never let passing it create false confidence.

There is also a secondary magnetic effect worth knowing: genuine gold and silver are slightly diamagnetic, meaning a very strong magnet held close will actually create a slight repulsion or drag rather than attraction. This is subtle and requires practice to detect, but experienced buyers can use it as an additional confirmation on larger pieces.

- **TEST 3: DIMENSION AND WEIGHT TESTING**

Test: #3 — Dimension and Weight Testing

Difficulty: Beginner to Intermediate

Equipment Cost: $20–40 for a quality digital scale and caliper

Catches: Wrong-weight fakes, wrong-size fakes, many plated base metal fakes

Limitation: Cannot catch tungsten-core fakes — tungsten's density is nearly identical to gold

---

Precious metals have specific densities, which means that for any given size there is a specific weight the piece should be. A genuine one-ounce Gold Eagle has an actual weight of thirty-three point nine three grams — heavier than its stated gold content because of the copper and silver alloy. Any significant deviation from published specifications is a red flag.

You need two pieces of equipment. First, a good digital caliper to measure diameter and thickness. Compare your measurements to published specifications for the specific coin — these are available on mint websites and reputable reference sources. Second, a digital scale that measures to at least zero point zero one grams precision. Weigh the coin and compare to published weight specifications.

The limitation is important to understand: tungsten-core fakes can match both dimensions and weight because tungsten's density is so close to gold's. This test eliminates many categories of fake but not the most sophisticated ones. Run it anyway — it catches a lot, it costs almost nothing, and it builds your hands-on familiarity with genuine coins in ways that have compounding value.

- **TEST 4: THE PING TEST (SOUND TEST)**

Test: #4 — The Ping Test (Sound Test)

Difficulty: Intermediate — requires practice

Equipment Cost: Free — or a few dollars for a coin testing app

Catches: Hollow fakes, wrong-metal cores, some tungsten fakes

Limitation: Requires practice to develop a reliable ear; less useful for bars

---

When you tap a genuine precious metal coin with another metal object and balance it on your fingertip, it produces a clear, sustained ring — a pure tone that fades slowly. Base metal coins and fakes with wrong-metal cores produce a dull, short thud. The difference, once you've heard both, is unmistakable.

To do this properly, balance the coin on your fingertip — not gripping it, which dampens the sound — and tap it gently on the edge with another coin or a pen. Let it ring freely. Gold coins have a distinctive bell-like tone. Silver rings even more clearly and at a higher pitch. A dull, dead sound tells you something is wrong.

Several smartphone apps can now analyze the sound frequency and compare it to database readings for known genuine coins. The apps aren't perfect, but they add objectivity to a test that otherwise requires developed ear. The Bullion Test app and similar tools are worth the modest cost for buyers who use this method regularly.

Tungsten's acoustic properties differ from gold — its ring is more metallic and less sustained — and experienced ears can detect well-made tungsten fakes this way. But the test requires genuine practice. Don't rely on it until you've handled enough genuine coins to have a reference point.

- **TEST 5: SPECIFIC GRAVITY TESTING**

Test: #5 — Specific Gravity Testing

Difficulty: Intermediate — requires care and proper setup

Equipment Cost: $30–60 for a hydrostatic weighing setup

Catches: Almost everything — highly effective including many tungsten fakes

Limitation: Time-consuming; requires precise technique; edge cases with alloys

---

Specific gravity — also called hydrostatic weighing — measures density by comparing an object's weight in air to its weight suspended in water. Since gold has a very specific density and tungsten is close but not identical, this test can detect tungsten cores that fool weight and dimension testing.

Here's how it works. Weigh the item normally in air. Then suspend it in a container of water using fine thread or a dedicated setup and weigh it again while submerged. The difference between the two weights, combined with the known density of water, lets you calculate the item's precise density. Gold's density is nineteen point three grams per cubic centimeter. Tungsten is eighteen point six. That difference —

close but not identical — is detectable with precise measurement.

This test is more involved but highly effective. The equipment is inexpensive — a precise digital scale, a small container, a suspension setup — and the mathematics are straightforward once you've done it a few times. For buyers who regularly purchase from non-standard sources, or who handle large bars where other tests are harder to apply, it's worth learning.

> *"Testing everything, just like the book taught me. Even from reputable dealers — always verify. Weight perfect, dimensions correct, magnet test passed, electronic scan confirms authenticity. PASS. Ready for secure storage."*

- **TEST 6: ELECTRONIC TESTING (SIGMA METALYTICS / XRF)**

Test: #6 — Electronic Testing (Sigma Metalytics / XRF)

Difficulty: Advanced — significant equipment investment

Equipment Cost: Around $1,100–1,200 for Sigma SM1601 Original Bullion Set; $10,000–50,000+ for XRF

Catches: Virtually everything including sophisticated tungsten-core fakes

Limitation: Cost; XRF requires trained operation; Sigma has some limitations on thick bars

---

This is where authentication moves from good to definitive. Electronic testing equipment reads the metal's actual electromagnetic or chemical properties rather than its physical dimensions — which means it can detect what the coin is made of, not just how big and heavy it is.

Sigma Metalytics testers use electromagnetic conductivity to verify precious metal content without damaging the product. Different metals conduct electricity differently at specific frequencies, and the Sigma reads those signatures and compares them to known genuine products. A genuine Gold Eagle produces a specific conductivity signature. Tungsten produces a different one. The Sigma knows the difference.

A Sigma tester will catch most sophisticated tungsten-core fakes, including many that pass all the physical tests. It's non-destructive — the coin never leaves your hand — and produces a clear pass or fail result in seconds. The entry-level model for most buyers is the Sigma SM1601 Original Bullion Set, which retails around $1,100–1,200. One important note: the SM1601 tests resistivity only — you must also test density separately using a scale and water, as described in the specific gravity section above. The combination of both tests gives you definitive authentication.

XRF analyzers — X-Ray Fluorescence devices — are the gold standard of precious metals authentication. They shoot X-rays into the metal and analyze the characteristic radiation emitted, revealing elemental composition to laboratory precision. An XRF will tell you not just whether the item is gold, but what karat it is and what the alloy composition is. They cannot be fooled by sophisticated plating because they read well below the surface.

XRF units cost tens of thousands of dollars and require trained operation, which is why most individual buyers won't own one. But many established dealers have them, and you should insist on XRF testing for high-value transactions — particularly large bars, which are the most commonly counterfeited form because the reward justifies the manufacturing investment. Any reputable dealer will perform this test at your request and most will do it without charge for significant purchases.

If the professional side of authentication interests you — hallmarking standards, assay office procedures, refinery testing protocols, and how the trade verifies metal at an institutional level — that world is covered in depth in my **Precious Metals Trade Guide,** more about that book latter... For now, the seven tests in this chapter give you everything an individual buyer needs. The Conclusion will tell you where to find the Trade Guide when you are ready for more.

- **TEST 7: ACID TESTING**

Test: #7 — Acid Testing

Difficulty: Intermediate — requires caution and care

Equipment Cost: $20–40 for a complete acid test kit

Catches: Surface gold content — detects plating and wrong-karat metal

Limitation: Destructive — leaves a small mark; tests surface only, not core

---

Acid testing has been used for centuries to verify gold and silver content. You make a tiny scratch on the item or rub it across a black basalt test stone, then apply a small drop of acid. Genuine gold at the correct karat resists the acid. Base metals and wrong-karat alloys react — dissolving, discoloring, or fizzing in ways that reveal their composition.

Different acid concentrations test for different gold karats — ten karat, fourteen karat, eighteen karat, twenty-two karat — so a complete kit includes multiple acids. The test is reliable for what it measures: the composition of the surface material. A plated coin will fail an acid test because the plating wears through quickly and the base metal beneath reacts to the acid.

The limitation is equally important: acid tests the surface, not the core. A tungsten coin with a thick enough gold shell can pass an acid test while failing electromagnetic testing. For coins, I generally recommend the other methods over acid testing because they're non-destructive and often more comprehensive. For scrap gold or items where you're genuinely uncertain about karat, acid testing is quick, cheap, and reliable for what it tells you.

WHEN TO DEMAND PROFESSIONAL VERIFICATION

For everyday bullion purchases from reputable dealers — established online companies or trusted local shops — the combination of visual inspection, magnet test, weight and dimensions, and a sound test is adequate for standard government coins. These dealers have reputations to protect and supply chains that trace back to legitimate mints. The residual risk is low, and your basic kit covers it.

But there are situations that demand more. Knowing when to escalate is as important as knowing the tests themselves.

Large purchases from unfamiliar sources require professional verification as a non-negotiable condition. If you're spending tens of thousands of dollars with a dealer you haven't worked with before, insist on Sigma or XRF testing before funds transfer. Any legitimate dealer will accommodate this. A dealer who resists has answered your question.

Private sales, estate purchases, and coin show transactions from unknown dealers call for maximum caution. Bring your testing kit. Use it on every piece. For significant amounts, consider a dealer intermediary who can provide authoritative authentication before you commit.

Large bars need professional testing as a rule, not an exception. A one-hundred-ounce silver bar or a kilo gold bar contains enough value to justify sophisticated counterfeiting, and the physical dimensions make some tests harder to apply. XRF testing on large bars is standard practice for serious buyers.

Trust your instincts about anything that feels wrong. If the price is better than it should be, if the seller seems nervous about verification, if something about the transaction creates discomfort you can't quite name — that discomfort is information. The cost of additional testing is trivial. The cost of being wrong is not.

YOUR AUTHENTICATION KIT — WHAT YOU ACTUALLY NEED

1. For buyers who purchase primarily from established dealers and stick to standard government coins: A strong neodymium magnet ($5–10) and a digital scale accurate to 0.01 grams ($25–40). These two tools, used on every purchase, catch the vast majority of fakes you're likely to encounter in normal buying from legitimate sources. Also download a coin ping app — free or a few dollars — and practice the sound test until you can hear the difference.
2. For buyers who attend coin shows, purchase from private sellers, or buy regularly from varied sources: Add a digital caliper ($15–25) for precise dimension checking and a specific gravity testing setup ($30–50). With these four tools you have a thorough physical testing capability that catches everything except the most sophisticated tungsten-core fakes.
3. For serious buyers who make regular significant purchases: Invest in a Sigma Metalytics SM1601 Original Bullion Set — around $1,100–1,200. This is the level of authentication that catches sophisticated tungsten-core fakes. It is non-destructive, fast, and straightforward to use. Pair it with specific gravity testing (scale plus water) for complete coverage. If

you are spending meaningful money regularly, this investment pays for itself on the first fake it catches — which it will, if you use it long enough.

4. For all buyers, always: Insist on XRF testing at the dealer's facility for any single purchase above your personal comfort threshold — whatever that number is. Established dealers have this equipment or access to it. Your request is normal, reasonable, and expected by any operation running a legitimate business.
5. The most important authentication tool is not a piece of equipment. It is the habit of always testing — every purchase, every time, from every source, without exception. Complacency is what counterfeits depend on. Remove the complacency and you remove most of the risk.

THE BOTTOM LINE ON COUNTERFEITS

Counterfeits exist. They are more sophisticated than they used to be. And they are relatively rare in normal buying from established sources — rare enough that many buyers go years without encountering one.

But rare is not zero. And the cost of encountering one without adequate authentication is not recoverable. Those tungsten Krugerrands would have cost me fifty thousand dollars. For most individual buyers, a single significant fake purchase would represent a devastating loss — not just of money, but of the security and peace of mind that was the whole point of owning precious metals in the first place.

The testing methods in this chapter are not about paranoia. They are about the rational management of a known risk at trivially low cost compared to the potential downside. A twenty-dollar magnet and a thirty-dollar scale, used consistently, will protect you from the overwhelming majority of counterfeits you're likely to encounter in a lifetime of normal buying. An eight-hundred-dollar electronic tester will protect you from essentially all of them.

Buy the equipment. Use it every time. That discipline, maintained without exception, is the single most reliable protection available to a precious metals buyer.

★ ***I verify the authenticity of every purchase using proper testing equipment — because trust without verification is not trust at all. It is wishful thinking.*** ★

COMING UP NEXT

A woman in Florida accumulated silver for eleven years — patient, methodical, well-priced. Everything stored in her basement in cardboard tubes. Then her basement flooded.

The silver survived. The documentation didn't. The insurance claim didn't. Chapter Six is about making sure everything you've done right stays intact when you need it: the safe specifications that actually matter, the insurance step most collectors skip, and the estate planning document that could save your family months of legal proceedings — and that almost nobody writes until it's too late.

CHAPTER SIX
STORAGE, SECURITY & THE ESTATE PLANNING PROBLEM

> *Buying the right metal at the right price from the right dealer and verifying it's genuine — none of that matters if you can't keep it, can't protect it, and your family can't find it when you're gone.*

Every week, somewhere in this country, a family discovers that a deceased relative owned precious metals. Sometimes they find it listed in an estate inventory. More often they don't — and the metals sit hidden or unaccounted for, occasionally for years, while family members argue over an estate that's missing assets nobody can locate.

I've watched this happen more times than I can count. A widow calls asking whether her late husband might have had gold, because she found a receipt in his files. A son reaches out because his father mentioned silver coins once, but nobody knows where they are. An attorney calls because probate is stalled over assets the family can't find or value.

This is the storage and estate planning problem in its most painful form. And it isn't caused by negligence or bad intent — it's caused by the same privacy instinct that makes precious metals owners keep their holdings quiet. The secrecy that protects living owners can devastate their families after they're gone.

This chapter covers the full storage picture: where to keep your metals, how to protect them from theft and disaster, how insurance works (and when it doesn't), and the estate planning steps that ensure everything you've built actually reaches the people you intended it for.

THE THREE THREATS YOU'RE PROTECTING AGAINST

Every storage decision is really a response to three distinct threats, and good storage addresses all three simultaneously. Understanding them separately helps you evaluate options clearly.

Theft is the most obvious threat and the one most people plan for. Someone takes your metal — whether by burglary, robbery, or in some cases fraud by people close to you. The protective response is physical security: weight, bolts, locks, concealment, and access control.

Disaster is the threat most people underestimate. Fire, flood, hurricane, earthquake — events that damage or destroy the physical space where metal is kept. Gold survives fire well because of its high melting point. Silver tarnishes but survives. Paper documents, plastic cases, and cardboard tubes do not — which means your records and provenance documentation face the same risk as less durable assets. The protective response is fire rating, waterproofing, elevation, and offsite redundancy.

Inaccessibility is the threat almost nobody considers until it's too late. Your metal exists, it's safe, nobody stole it — but nobody who needs to access it can. You're incapacitated. You're deceased. The combination to your safe is in your head and nowhere else. Your family doesn't know the metal exists, or knows it exists but has no idea where. The protective response is documentation, communication, and estate planning.

The best storage solution addresses all three. A safe that nobody knows about protects against theft but creates an inaccessibility problem. A bank safe deposit box protects against theft and some disasters but creates access problems when the owner is incapacitated. A documented inventory shared with family addresses inaccessibility but creates a security risk if that information reaches the wrong people.

Navigating these competing concerns is the real challenge of precious metals storage. Let's go through your options.

HOME STORAGE: DOING IT RIGHT

Home storage is the most common choice and, done correctly, a legitimate one. Done incorrectly, it's a disaster waiting to happen in one of several forms.

The Safe: Your Non-Negotiable Foundation

If you store precious metals at home, you need a quality safe. Not a fireproof box from the hardware store. Not a drawer lock or hidden compartment as your primary security. A real safe — heavy, bolted, rated.

Weight matters enormously. A safe that can be carried out by two people will be carried out by two people. The minimum weight for a home safe that provides meaningful burglary protection is three hundred pounds. Five hundred pounds is better. Above that, the safe is extremely difficult to move even with equipment, especially if it's also anchored.

Anchoring is the other half of the weight equation. A five-hundred-pound safe bolted to concrete with proper anchor bolts is a serious obstacle. The same safe sitting unanchored on a wooden floor can be tipped, pried, and eventually moved with enough time and effort. Install the anchor bolts. Follow the manufacturer's specifications. Hire a professional if you're not confident doing it yourself — the cost is trivial relative to what you're protecting.

UL ratings tell you what independent testing has verified. Look for a UL Residential Security Container rating for burglary resistance and a fire rating expressed in hours and internal temperature. A one-hour fire rating means the interior temperature stays below the paper ignition point for one hour in a standard fire — adequate for most residential fires. Two hours provides more margin.

Location matters as much as the safe itself. The obvious location — the master bedroom — is also the first place any experienced burglar goes. A utility room, basement corner, closet in a less-trafficked part of the house, or a purpose-built vault room all provide better security through concealment. The goal is for a burglar who has entered your home to not immediately know where the safe is and not have easy access to it without being heard.

> *"Five hundred pounds, bolted to concrete, UL-rated for burglary and fire. Installed in the utility room — not the obvious bedroom location. Even if someone breaks in, they won't know where to look.*

Once these anchor bolts are in, this safe isn't going anywhere."

What Not to Do

The most common home storage mistakes are predictable enough that burglars count on them. A small fireproof box on a closet shelf. A floor safe with a thin carpet square over it. A safe in the master bedroom closet. Metals wrapped in cloth inside a drawer. A combination written on a sticky note attached to the safe itself.

None of these are adequate. Each one is a version of a known pattern that experienced thieves recognize and exploit within minutes. If your current storage arrangement fits any of these descriptions, treat this chapter as an urgent action item rather than background reading.

THE DISASTER PROBLEM: WHAT FIRE AND FLOOD ACTUALLY DO

Margaret had been collecting silver for eleven years. American Silver Eagles, pre-1965 junk silver, a few silver bars — methodically accumulated and stored in her basement in a combination of cardboard coin tubes and plastic storage bins. Everything was documented in a spiral notebook she kept with the collection.

Then her basement flooded after an unusually heavy storm. Two feet of water, standing for nearly eighteen hours before it pumped out. The silver itself survived — gold and silver don't corrode in water the way base metals do. But the cardboard tubes disintegrated. The plastic bins floated and overturned. The spiral notebook dissolved into illegible pulp. Her insurance adjuster reviewed the claim and denied it: the policy excluded water damage to valuables stored in spaces without waterproofing measures, and the storage method — cardboard, open bins — didn't meet the policy's definition of proper containment.

She lost her documentation, her provenance records, her purchase history, and her insurance claim. The metal was still there, but years of careful record-keeping vanished in a night.

> *"Ten thousand dollars in silver — ruined. Stored in cardboard boxes in the basement. I never thought about flooding risk. Should have used waterproof containers, elevated storage, or a bank box. The insurance adjuster said the policy doesn't cover water damage to improperly stored valuables. Insurance won't cover this — improper storage voids my policy."*

Gold and silver are physically resilient. They survive fire better than most materials and survive water indefinitely. What doesn't survive are the things around them: packaging, documentation, storage containers, and the records that establish provenance and value for insurance and estate purposes.

Protect against disaster with three measures. First, use waterproof containers — airtight capsules, sealed tubes, dry boxes — not cardboard or paper. Second, keep your collection elevated off the floor in any space with flood risk. Third, and most importantly, keep your documentation somewhere other than with the metal. Scanned records stored in secure cloud backup, copies with your attorney, a second set in a bank safe deposit box — any of these ensures your records survive events that damage your storage location.

Fire protection for the metal itself is less urgent than most people assume — gold melts at nearly two thousand degrees Fahrenheit, and residential fires rarely reach that sustained temperature. But a fire-rated safe protects against the heat damage that can affect silver's finish and destroys all the paper around your collection.

! STORAGE MISTAKES THAT VOID INSURANCE COVERAGE

1. Storing in cardboard, paper tubes, or unsealed containers in flood-prone spaces. Most homeowner and rider policies require proper containment. Check your policy's specific language before assuming coverage.
2. Exceeding declared value limits without updating your policy. A collection that has grown significantly

since you last spoke with your insurer may be partially or entirely uninsured for the current value.

3. No documentation of what you own. Claims require proof of ownership and value. Without purchase receipts, photographs, and an inventory, your insurer has no basis to pay a claim — and the burden of proof is entirely on you.
4. Failure to declare precious metals as a specific category. Standard homeowner's policies typically cap precious metals coverage at $1,000–2,500. Without a specific rider or floater policy, most collections are dramatically underinsured.
5. Storing in a location excluded by your policy. Many policies exclude outbuildings, detached garages, storage units, or specific rooms. Verify that your storage location is covered before assuming it is.

INSURANCE: WHAT YOU ACTUALLY NEED

Standard homeowner's insurance is almost never adequate for a meaningful precious metals collection. The typical policy caps coverage for precious metals, coins, and bullion at somewhere between one thousand and twenty-five hundred dollars — a figure that covers a fraction of even a modest collection.

To be properly insured, you need either a scheduled personal property endorsement or a standalone precious metals floater policy. A scheduled endorsement adds specific items — or an entire collection valued as a whole — to your homeowner's policy at an agreed value. A standalone floater covers the collection specifically, often with broader coverage terms than a homeowner's endorsement.

Either approach requires documentation. Your insurer will want a current inventory with values, purchase receipts where available, and often an independent appraisal for high-value items. This documentation burden is not an obstacle — it's an opportunity. The process of documenting your collection for insurance creates exactly the records your estate will need, and having agreed value coverage eliminates the negotiation that otherwise follows a claim.

Get quotes from insurers who specialize in collectibles and precious metals — they understand the market better than general insurers and typically offer better terms. Review your coverage annually as your collection grows and as precious metals prices change. A collection insured for its value two years ago may be significantly underinsured today if prices have risen substantially.

One more thing: ask your insurer specifically about coverage for metal stored in bank safe deposit boxes and for metal in transit. Both situations have coverage implications that differ from in-home storage, and both matter if you move metal between locations.

PROFESSIONAL STORAGE: VAULTS AND DEPOSITORIES

Professional precious metals storage — dedicated vault facilities operated by established bullion dealers or independent storage companies — offers security and insurance levels that home storage cannot match, at costs that are modest relative to the value being protected.

A reputable bullion depository provides segregated or allocated storage, meaning your specific metal is set aside for you rather than pooled with others' holdings. You receive regular statements confirming your holdings. The facility carries substantial insurance. Physical security exceeds anything practical in a home environment. And your metal is accessible on reasonable notice without requiring you to manage the security logistics yourself.

The trade-off is that your metal is not immediately in your hands, which matters to some buyers and not at all to others. For a wealth preserver holding gold as long-term financial insurance, professional storage often makes more practical sense than home storage. For a buyer who values the tangibility of personal possession and wants immediate physical access, home storage has appeal that no monthly statement can replace.

If you use professional storage, verify the facility's insurance coverage, confirm the storage is segregated rather than pooled, understand the terms for taking physical delivery, and ensure your estate documentation includes account information and access instructions. A professionally stored collection that your heirs cannot locate or access is only marginally better than one hidden at home without documentation.

BANK SAFE DEPOSIT BOXES: USEFUL BUT LIMITED

Bank safe deposit boxes provide excellent physical security at very low cost, and many precious metals owners use them for a portion of their holdings — particularly for irreplaceable items, important documentation, or metal they don't anticipate needing immediate access to.

The limitations are real and worth understanding. Safe deposit boxes are not insured by the FDIC — bank deposit accounts are, but box contents are not. You need your own insurance rider. Boxes are only accessible during banking hours, which matters if you need your metal quickly during a bank holiday or extended closure. If the bank fails, box access can be restricted during resolution proceedings. And if you're the sole signatory and become incapacitated, your family may face legal hurdles accessing the box even in urgent circumstances.

The practical solution for many buyers is a combination approach: meaningful home storage in a quality safe for working holdings and immediate access needs, with a safe deposit box holding documentation, a secondary inventory record, and perhaps a portion of the collection as offsite backup.

THE ESTATE PLANNING PROBLEM NOBODY TALKS ABOUT

Here is the uncomfortable truth that most precious metals books never address directly: a significant percentage of privately held precious metals is never recovered by intended heirs.

Some of it is lost outright — hidden in locations the owner forgot or couldn't communicate before dying. Some sits unrecovered because heirs don't know it exists. Some is found but can't be properly valued or liquidated because there's no documentation of what it is or where it came from. And some becomes the subject of family disputes because the owner's intentions were never clearly expressed.

This isn't a small problem. Precious metals are uniquely vulnerable to this fate because their owners deliberately keep them private, store them in non-obvious locations, and often treat their holdings as personal rather than estate matters. The privacy instinct that protects a living owner can devastate the estate left to their family.

> ***The question is not whether your family will eventually find out about your precious metals holdings. The question is whether they'll find out while you're alive and can guide them — or after you're gone, when guidance is no longer possible and the estate is already in motion.***

What Your Estate Needs to Know

Your estate planning for precious metals needs to cover four things: what you own, where it is, how to access it, and what to do with it.

What you own means a current inventory: each item by type, weight, quantity, mint, year where relevant, and approximate current value. This inventory should be updated at least annually and whenever you make significant additions. It should exist in written form, in a location your executor knows about.

Where it is means specific location information — which safe, which bank and box number, which depository account. If you use a combination safe, the combination needs to be documented somewhere your executor can find it after your death but a burglar cannot find it during your lifetime. This is a genuine tension that requires a thoughtful solution: a sealed envelope held by your attorney, instructions in your will that reference a location your executor is separately informed of, or a trusted family member who holds the combination with clear instructions about when to use it.

How to access it means the practical steps your heirs need to take — account numbers, dealer contact information, the process for liquidating or transferring specific types of holdings. Silver Eagles liquidate differently than a large gold bar. Dealer relationships matter for getting fair value. Your heirs shouldn't have to figure this out from scratch under the stress of estate administration.

What to do with it is optional but valuable — your expressed wishes about whether holdings should be distributed in kind to specific heirs, liquidated and added to the general estate, or handled in some other way. Without expressed wishes, your executor must make these decisions without guidance, and family members may have strong and conflicting opinions.

> *"My precious metals won't help my family if they can't find them or access them. Clear instructions ensure they benefit from what I've built. Storage locations, access codes, dealer contacts, inventory — everything they need to claim and manage these assets properly. I plan ahead so my precious metals benefit those I love most."*

The Practical Document: Your Precious Metals Letter

The most useful estate planning tool for precious metals owners is a simple, clearly written letter addressed to your executor and heirs. Not a legal document — just a plain-language account of everything they need to know.

This letter should be stored in a location your executor is informed about — with your attorney, in your safe deposit box, or in a clearly labeled envelope in your home files. It should be updated whenever significant changes occur. And it should be specific enough that a person with no prior knowledge of your holdings could locate, identify, access, and appropriately handle everything you own.

Include the location of every storage point, with access instructions for each. List every account — bank boxes, depository accounts, any other financial arrangements related to your metals. Name your primary dealer contacts and explain the nature of those relationships. Describe your collection in enough detail that your heirs understand what they have. And note any wishes you have about distribution or handling.

This letter is not part of your will and doesn't need to be. It's practical guidance from you to the people who will handle your affairs — the kind of guidance that transforms a complicated estate problem into a manageable task.

YOUR STORAGE & ESTATE PLANNING CHECKLIST

1. If you store metals at home: verify your safe weighs at least 300 pounds, is properly anchored to concrete or structural framing, is UL-rated for burglary resistance, and is located somewhere other than the master

bedroom. If any of these conditions isn't met, correct it before your next purchase.

2. Check your homeowner's insurance policy right now. Find the section covering precious metals, coins, and bullion. Note the coverage limit. If that limit is less than your current collection's replacement value, call your insurer this week and ask about a scheduled endorsement or floater policy. Bring your inventory.
3. Create or update your collection inventory — every item, quantity, weight, approximate value, purchase source where known. Store this document somewhere separate from your collection: scanned and backed up digitally, with a physical copy at your attorney's office or in your safe deposit box.
4. Write your precious metals letter. Where everything is. How to access it. Who to call. What your wishes are. Put it in a sealed envelope labeled clearly. Tell your executor exactly where to find it. Update it whenever your holdings change significantly.
5. If your metal is in a bank safe deposit box and you are the sole signatory: add a trusted person as co-signatory, or ensure your estate documents specifically grant your executor authority to access the box without a court order. Research your state's specific requirements — they vary significantly.
6. Review your storage and documentation annually. Precious metals values change. Your collection grows. Your family circumstances evolve. What was adequate documentation two years ago may leave gaps today. Set a calendar reminder and treat this review as seriously as you treat reviewing your other financial accounts.

★ ***My metals are properly secured, properly insured, and properly documented — so they protect my family both during my lifetime and long after.*** ★

COMING UP NEXT

Raymond put forty thousand dollars into silver in spring 2011. He'd been watching the market for two years, waiting for the right moment. When everyone around him was finally talking about silver, he decided certainty had arrived. Six months later, silver had dropped more than forty percent.

He'd done nothing wrong with his products or his dealer. He'd done everything wrong with his timing and his psychology. Chapter Seven is the discipline playbook: how to build a position steadily over years, how to recognize the market conditions that have historically trapped buyers like Raymond, and how to make sure patience — not a single bad decision — defines your outcome.

CHAPTER SEVEN

BUILDING YOUR POSITION OVER TIME

> *Knowing what to buy is only half the equation. Knowing how to build a position steadily, without emotional decisions, without overpaying at the wrong moment, and without taking on more risk than your situation warrants — that's what separates successful long-term owners from buyers who end up disappointed.*

Raymond came to see me in the spring of 2011. Silver had been climbing steadily for months, the financial media was breathless about it, and Raymond had just put forty thousand dollars into silver at prices near their all-time peak. He'd been watching the market for two years, waiting for the right moment, and when everyone around him seemed to be talking about silver he decided the time had finally come.

He was in my shop six months later. Silver had dropped more than forty percent from its peak. He wanted to know what he'd done wrong.

He hadn't done anything wrong with his product choice. The silver he bought was genuine, properly priced at the time of purchase, and from a reputable dealer. What he'd done wrong was let the market's excitement drive his timing. He'd waited for certainty — the kind of certainty that only arrives at the top of a market, when everyone has already bought and there are no new buyers left to push prices higher.

Raymond's story is common enough that it has a name in market history. But it doesn't have to be your story. The approach in this chapter — systematic, disciplined, emotion-resistant — exists precisely to keep buyers out of the trap Raymond fell into.

YOUR GOAL DETERMINES YOUR APPROACH

Before any discussion of how to build a position, you need clarity on why you're building it. The right accumulation strategy for a wealth preserver holding gold as a twenty-year financial backstop looks nothing like the right approach for an investor with a five-year horizon or a prepper focused on silver's barter utility.

The wealth preserver's primary goal is preserving purchasing power across decades. Time is their greatest asset — short-term price swings are irrelevant, and the only question that matters is whether gold will preserve value better than cash or bonds over a generation. For this buyer, a simple, consistent accumulation plan maintained through all market conditions is almost certainly the right approach.

The investor with a medium-term horizon cares more about entry price relative to likely exit price. Round-trip costs matter more. Position sizing matters more. The investor needs to think about what conditions would cause them to sell and what return they need to justify the round-trip cost calculated in Chapter Four.

The prepper focused on silver's practical utility thinks differently again — about specific coin formats, about divisibility for barter, about storage quantities that match plausible scenarios. Their accumulation logic is driven by use cases rather than financial return.

Most buyers are some combination of these types, which is fine. But be honest with yourself about your primary motivation. It determines your time horizon, which determines how much short-term volatility you should be willing to accept, which determines how aggressively you should buy during price dips and how calmly you should sit through price drops.

DOLLAR COST AVERAGING: THE DISCIPLINE THAT WORKS

Dollar cost averaging is the practice of investing a fixed dollar amount at regular intervals regardless of price. It is not a sophisticated strategy. It requires no market knowledge, no price forecasting ability, and no emotional discipline beyond the decision to keep going when the market makes you want to stop.

Its power comes from a simple mathematical reality: when you invest a fixed dollar amount, you buy more units when prices are low and fewer when prices are high. Over time, this produces an average cost per unit that is lower than the average price over the same period. You don't need to predict where prices are going. You just need to keep buying.

For precious metals specifically, dollar cost averaging has additional advantages beyond the mathematical ones. It removes the timing decision entirely — the decision that cost Raymond forty thousand dollars of opportunity and months of anxiety. It keeps premiums manageable by avoiding the panic-premium spikes that accompany everyone else's surge buying. And it builds the habit of consistent accumulation that, over years and decades, produces positions of genuine substance.

The practical implementation is straightforward. Choose a fixed amount — whatever fits your budget without creating financial strain. Choose a fixed interval — monthly works well for most people because it aligns with income cycles. Choose your preferred product and dealer. Then execute on schedule regardless of what gold or silver is doing that month.

That last part is the only hard part. When prices drop, the instinct is to pause — to wait for the bottom before buying more. When prices rise, the instinct is to accelerate — to buy more before prices go higher. Both instincts work against you. The drop that makes you want to pause is exactly the moment your fixed purchase buys the most metal. The rise that makes you want to accelerate is exactly the moment your fixed purchase buys the least.

> *"Month twelve of consistent buying. Sometimes prices are up, sometimes down — but I'm averaging in over time and building real wealth. No trying to time the market, no emotional decisions. Just $500 every month like clockwork. The discipline is working."*

Setting Up Your DCA Plan

A workable dollar cost averaging plan needs three decisions made in advance: how much, how often, and what to buy.

How much is a personal financial question, not a precious metals question. The right amount is one that leaves your emergency fund intact, doesn't require you to carry credit card debt to fund, and won't cause you genuine financial hardship in a difficult month. Starting smaller and maintaining the plan is vastly better than starting larger and abandoning it when circumstances change. Many successful accumulators start at two hundred or three hundred dollars a month and increase the amount gradually as their financial situation allows.

How often is mostly a question of convenience and transaction cost. Monthly is the most common interval and aligns naturally with most people's income and expense cycles. Quarterly works for buyers who prefer fewer transactions or whose budgets are less predictable. Weekly works for some buyers who want smoother averaging. Avoid intervals so short that transaction costs and minimum order sizes become friction — if your chosen amount is smaller than a dealer's minimum order, adjust the interval.

What to buy should be decided in advance and changed infrequently. A single product, bought consistently from a single reliable dealer, simplifies everything — authentication is familiar, storage is consistent, and selling is straightforward because you know exactly what you have. Many consistent accumulators buy one-ounce Gold Eagles, or American Silver Eagles, or a combination of both in a fixed ratio. The specific product matters less than the consistency of the plan.

POSITION SIZING: HOW MUCH IS RIGHT FOR YOU

How large should your precious metals position be relative to your overall financial picture? This is one of the questions I'm asked most often, and the answer is genuinely personal — which means the generic answers you hear are worth examining critically.

The commonly cited guideline of five to ten percent of investable assets in precious metals has been around for decades and reflects a reasonable allocation for a wealth preserver who already has other assets — retirement accounts, real estate, cash reserves — providing different forms of financial security. It's not a law of physics. It's a starting point for thinking.

Consider the five to ten percent range as a ballpark for someone whose primary goal is long-term wealth preservation alongside other assets. If your situation is different — if precious metals represent a more central part of your financial strategy, or if you're in a period of genuine economic concern and want more insurance — a higher allocation may make sense. If you're just beginning and want to understand the market before committing significant capital, a lower starting allocation is entirely rational.

What matters more than the exact percentage is the relationship between your metals position and your liquidity. Precious metals are not instantly liquid in the way a bank account or money market fund is. Selling takes time — finding a buyer, completing the transaction, receiving payment. Your metals position should never be money you might need in the next thirty to sixty days. It should represent capital you can genuinely afford to hold for years, because that's what the asset is designed for.

The other sizing consideration is concentration risk. A portfolio that is ninety percent precious metals is not a diversified portfolio — it's a concentrated bet on one asset class, however historically reliable that asset class may be. Even gold has extended periods of flat or declining prices when held in nominal terms. A position large enough to provide meaningful protection is very different from a position so large it creates the anxiety it was supposed to relieve.

REBALANCING: KEEPING YOUR POSITION IN PROPORTION

As precious metals prices change over time, their percentage of your overall portfolio shifts. Gold rising forty percent in a strong year might push your allocation from eight percent to twelve percent. Gold falling twenty percent might push it from eight percent to six.

Rebalancing means periodically adjusting back toward your target allocation — selling some of your metals position when it has grown significantly above target, or buying more when it has fallen significantly below. This is not market timing. It's the mechanical application of a predetermined rule that forces you to take some profit when prices are high and buy more when prices are low — the opposite of what emotion drives most people to do.

For most individual investors, annual rebalancing is sufficient. Check your allocation once a year. If precious metals have grown to more than five percentage points above your target, consider trimming. If they've fallen more than five points below target, consider adding. Keep the decisions mechanical and predetermined rather than reactive to whatever the market has been doing recently.

Rebalancing also provides a natural framework for the question of when to sell. Rather than trying to pick a top — an exercise in futility that has humbled professional investors for generations — you sell incrementally as the position grows above target. This captures some gains without requiring you to make a prediction about future prices.

TIMING: WHAT YOU CAN CONTROL AND WHAT YOU CAN'T

You cannot consistently predict where gold or silver prices will be next month or next year. Neither can I, and neither can the analysts who sell newsletters claiming they can. The track record of short-term precious metals forecasting is poor enough that treating any such forecast as actionable is its own form of risk.

What you can control is the premium you pay, which is significantly influenced by when and how you buy. Premiums are tightest when markets are calm and demand is moderate — the times when nobody is talking about precious metals at a dinner party. Premiums spike when demand surges during market panics or periods of intense media attention. Buying during calm periods and avoiding panic purchases is the single most controllable timing decision available to you.

You can also control which part of a cycle you accumulate in. Precious metals move in long cycles — periods of significant appreciation followed by extended periods of flat or declining prices. You cannot time these cycles with precision, but you can recognize the extremes. When every mainstream financial commentator is bullish on gold, when television advertising for precious metals is ubiquitous, when your barber and dentist are talking about buying silver — those are historically reliable signs that the easy gains have already occurred and caution is warranted.

> *"Gold dropped in two weeks — but I'm not panicking. I'm preserving wealth for 10–20 years, not trading monthly moves. This is exactly the volatility the book warned about. My thesis hasn't changed — inflation protection, currency insurance, long-term store of*

value. Short-term noise doesn't change the long-term thesis."

The inverse is equally true. When precious metals are out of fashion, when financial media ignores them, when buyers are scarce and dealer inventory is abundant — that's historically when patient buyers have built their best positions. The difficulty is that these periods feel uncomfortable precisely because nothing seems to be happening. Consistent accumulation through boring markets is where most long-term gains are actually built.

THE 1980 LESSON: WHAT MANIA COSTS

January 1980 remains the most instructive single event in modern precious metals history for individual buyers. Silver reached fifty dollars per ounce. Gold reached eight hundred fifty dollars. Both represented genuine all-time highs driven by a confluence of forces — inflation, geopolitical tension, the Hunt Brothers' attempt to corner the silver market, and the momentum buying of retail investors who had watched prices rise for years and couldn't imagine them falling.

They fell. Silver lost eighty percent of its value within a year. Gold fell sixty percent. And the buyers who purchased at or near the January 1980 peak — many of them ordinary people responding to exactly the kind of media frenzy and social excitement that characterizes market tops — waited thirty-one years for silver to return to fifty dollars. Thirty-one years. Many of them never saw it.

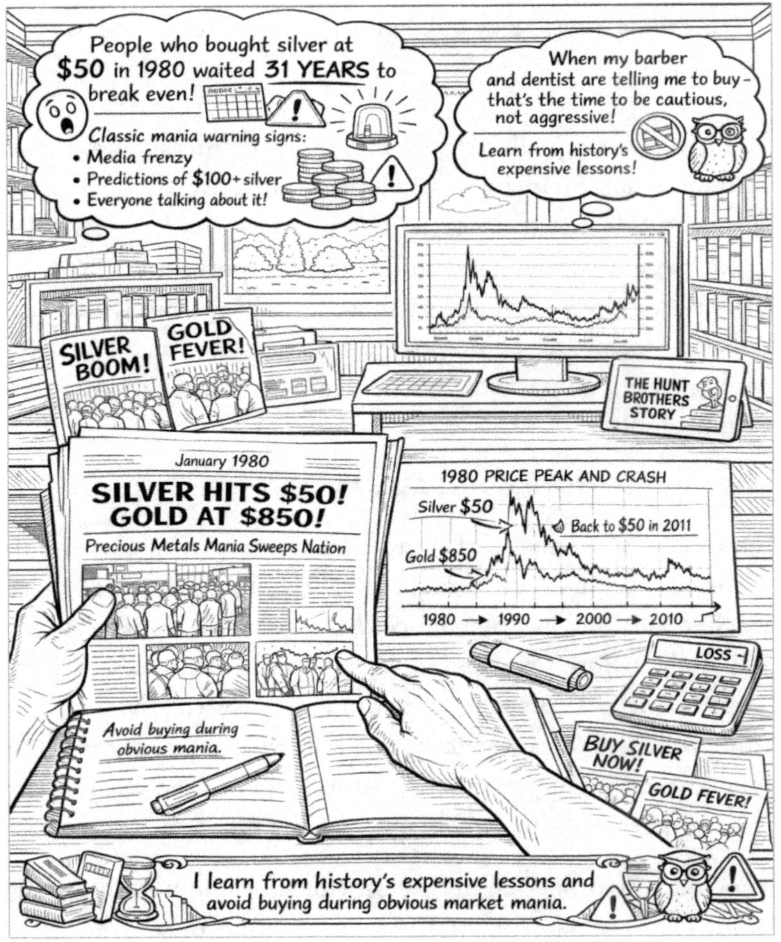

> *"People who bought silver at $50 in 1980 waited 31 years to break even. Classic mania warning signs: media frenzy, predictions of $100+ silver, everyone talking about it. When my barber and dentist are telling me to buy — that's the time to be cautious, not aggressive. Learn from history's expensive lessons. Avoid buying during obvious mania."*

This is not an argument against buying precious metals. It is an argument against buying them during obvious mania — when prices are driven by excitement and momentum rather than the underlying fundamentals that make gold and silver valuable as long-term stores of wealth.

The practical lesson for today's buyer is simple: when precious metals feel urgent and exciting, when the headlines make them seem like the obvious investment everyone should be making, slow down. Maintain your regular DCA purchases — don't suspend them — but resist the impulse to accelerate dramatically. The urgency you feel is not information about future prices. It's information about current sentiment, and peak sentiment is a historically reliable contrary indicator.

Conversely, when precious metals feel irrelevant and boring, when nobody seems interested and prices have been flat for years, that is frequently the time when patient accumulation builds the most valuable positions. The boredom is uncomfortable. That's precisely what makes the opportunity real.

! SIGNS YOU MAY BE BUYING AT THE WRONG TIME

1. Everyone around you is talking about gold or silver — at dinner, at work, in casual conversation. Broad retail enthusiasm for any asset class is historically a late-cycle indicator, not an early one. The smart money has usually already bought by the time the barber is recommending precious metals.
2. Television and radio advertising for precious metals is unusually heavy. Advertising spend tracks demand. Heavy advertising to retail buyers indicates elevated demand, which typically means elevated premiums

and elevated prices — the opposite of ideal buying conditions.

3. Predictions of dramatic, unprecedented price targets are everywhere. '$5,000 gold' and '$200 silver' headlines are a regular feature of market tops. Not because those prices are impossible, but because extreme price predictions attract attention precisely when prices are already extended.
4. You feel a sense of urgency — that you're missing something, that you need to buy more right now before it's too late. This emotional urgency is the opposite of the calm, deliberate accumulation that produces good long-term outcomes. When you feel urgency, pause and review your plan rather than acting on the feeling.
5. You're considering borrowing money to buy precious metals, selling other assets under pressure to fund a larger purchase, or making a single large purchase far outside your normal accumulation pattern. None of these reflect disciplined position building. All of them represent emotional responses to market conditions that have historically produced poor outcomes.

WHEN TO SELL: THE QUESTION NOBODY ASKS IN ADVANCE

Most precious metals buyers think carefully about when and how to buy. Very few think equally carefully about when and how to sell — until they find themselves holding a position and wondering whether current prices represent an opportunity or a peak.

Having a predetermined sell framework is not pessimism about precious metals. It's the same discipline that governs good accumulation. Just as you buy according to a plan rather than on emotion, you should sell according to a plan rather than on emotion.

For a wealth preserver, the question of selling is mostly a rebalancing question — trimming when the position grows significantly above target allocation, not liquidating. The long-term holder generally isn't looking for an exit; they're managing the size of an ongoing position.

For the investor with a specific horizon or return target, the framework is different. Define in advance what conditions would cause you to sell — a specific price target, a specific return on investment, a specific change in the economic conditions that motivated the purchase. Write it down. Review it annually. Having that framework prevents you from letting a winning position ride past your original thesis or selling a losing position in panic.

The universal sell trigger that applies to all buyer types: if your reason for owning precious metals has fundamentally changed — if the economic conditions you were protecting against have resolved, if your financial situation has changed and you need the capital — that's a legitimate reason to sell regardless of current prices. Holding an asset past the point where it serves its original purpose is as much an emotional decision as selling in panic. The plan should govern both.

This Playbook covers physical bullion ownership from first purchase to long-term position building. If you want to go further — into futures contracts, ETFs, mining shares, and how the professional trading world uses precious metals — those topics are covered comprehensively in the **Precious Metals Trade Guide**. The Conclusion tells you exactly where to find it and why I consider it the essential companion to everything you have learned here.

YOUR POSITION-BUILDING CHECKLIST

1. Write down your primary goal for owning precious metals — wealth preservation, investment return, practical preparedness, or some combination. Be specific. This goal determines your time horizon, your target allocation, and your response to price volatility. A goal you haven't written down is one you'll reinterpret in your favor when the market makes you uncomfortable.
2. Set your monthly (or quarterly) DCA amount at a level you can sustain without financial strain through a year of flat or declining prices. The right amount is the one you'll actually maintain when the market isn't cooperating, not the amount that feels right when you're excited about the asset class.
3. Decide your target allocation as a percentage of investable assets and write it down alongside your rebalancing rules — at what deviation from target you will add or trim. Review this allocation annually alongside your other financial accounts.
4. Identify your preferred product and primary dealer in advance. One-ounce government bullion coins from an established dealer are the standard choice for most consistent accumulators. Having this decision already made removes friction from each purchase and keeps you from reconsidering the basics every month.
5. Write your sell framework: what conditions would cause you to sell part or all of your position, and at what allocation level would you trim versus

maintain? A framework written during calm times will serve you better than a decision made under the pressure of a moving market.

6. Note the current market sentiment level. Is precious metals a topic of mainstream media enthusiasm right now? Are premiums elevated above normal ranges? If yes, consider maintaining your regular DCA pace but resisting any urge to accelerate. If the market is quiet and boring and premiums are tight — that's typically the better time to consider adding to your position above your regular pace.

★ ***I accumulate on a schedule, not on a feeling. Raymond bought when everyone was certain. I buy when the plan says to buy — regardless of what the market, the news, or anyone's certainty is telling me.*** ★

COMING UP NEXT

You've made it through the full playbook. What remains is putting it all together — a clear summary of the principles that govern intelligent precious metals ownership, and the mindset that will serve you across decades of market cycles, price swings, and economic uncertainty.

The Conclusion isn't a review. It's a letter from sixty years of experience to the buyer you're about to become.

CONCLUSION
A LETTER FROM SIXTY YEARS

You've done something most people who are interested in precious metals never do. You've read the whole book before spending the first dollar. That patience is already evidence of the temperament that makes a successful long-term owner.

I want to close with something more personal than a summary, because summaries are for people who skimmed and want the highlights. You read it. What you need now isn't the highlights repeated — it's a sense of where all of this knowledge fits into the longer story of why any of it matters.

I've been in this business for over sixty years. I've seen things that would astonish a new buyer and things that would confirm everything a new buyer fears. I've watched fortunes built quietly over decades by people who understood what precious metals are for and held them accordingly. I've watched good people lose significant money because they were sold a vision of easy profit instead of the reality of patient wealth preservation.

The difference between those two groups was almost never intelligence. It was almost never wealth or sophistication. It was knowledge — specific, practical, unglamorous knowledge about how this market actually works, who profits from buyer ignorance, and how to avoid the predictable traps that have been catching buyers since long before I started on Maxwell Street.

That knowledge is what this book contains. Not every question you'll ever have about precious metals — that would take several books and a career — but the foundation that lets you ask the right questions, evaluate the answers you receive, and make decisions that serve your actual interests rather than someone else's sales commission.

WHAT YOU NOW KNOW

You know that most people who walk into a precious metals purchase without preparation belong to one of four buyer types — and that knowing which type you are shapes every decision that follows. The wealth preserver, the investor, the collector, the prepper each have different needs and different vulnerabilities. You know which category fits you best, which means you know which pitfalls to watch for most carefully.

You know that the precious metals market has no universal standard of practice and no regulatory framework that protects buyers the way securities law protects investors. You are responsible for your own due diligence in a way that doesn't apply when you buy a stock or a mutual fund. That responsibility is not a burden — it's simply the reality, and knowing it is the first step to meeting it.

You know what to buy and why: government-issued bullion coins in standard sizes, from established mints, purchased at premiums that reflect fair market compensation for the manufacturing and distribution costs rather than the marketing budgets of television dealers. You know what to avoid and why those products look appealing to the uninformed: the numismatic trap, the rare coin pitch, the painted and commemorative products that carry premiums their resale value will never justify.

You know how to find a dealer worth trusting, what questions to ask before any money changes hands, and which answers should send you to the next dealer on your list. You know what Patricia's mistake was — and more importantly, you know exactly how to avoid making it yourself.

You know what spot price is, how premiums work, what the spread costs you, and how to calculate the round-trip cost of any transaction before you commit. You know which dealer is genuinely competitive and which one is charging you for their advertising budget. You know that the number on the price tag is never the number that determines whether a purchase makes financial sense.

You know how to verify what you buy — from the twenty-dollar magnet that costs nothing to run, to the specific gravity calculation that catches most tungsten fakes, to the electronic probe that is as close to definitive as individual buyers can get. You know that authentication is a habit, not an occasional courtesy, and you know exactly what equipment you need for the way you buy.

You know how to protect what you own: the safe specifications that matter, the location decisions that separate adequate security from wishful thinking, the insurance steps that ensure a claim can actually be paid. And you know the estate planning piece that almost nobody discusses — the letter your heirs will desperately need and that you are now equipped to write.

You know how to build a position over time without letting emotion drive your decisions — how to accumulate steadily when the market is boring, how to stay calm when it isn't, and how to recognize the signs of a market top that historically trap the buyers who act on excitement rather than discipline.

> ***Knowledge is the only protection in this market that cannot be taken from you. Everything else — the metal, the safe, the insurance policy — can be lost, stolen, or voided. What you understand about how this market works goes with you into every transaction you will ever make.***

THE LESSON THAT TOOK SIXTY YEARS

If I could distill everything I've learned into a single principle, it would be this: precious metals reward patience and punish impatience in almost every form.

Patience in accumulation — building a position over years rather than making a single large purchase at what feels like the right moment. Patience in holding — resisting the urge to sell during corrections that feel catastrophic but prove temporary. Patience in buying — waiting for reasonable premiums rather than panic-buying when the market makes everyone feel urgent. Patience in finding good dealers rather than accepting the first price quoted. Patience in learning rather than acting before you understand what you're doing.

Every expensive mistake I've seen made in this market was a form of impatience. The buyers who sent wire transfers to dealers they'd found online and never verified. The buyers who purchased numismatic coins because a persuasive salesman made them feel they'd miss out if they waited. The buyers who accelerated their purchasing dramatically at market tops because prices were rising and they wanted more. Raymond with his forty thousand dollars. Barbara with her eighty thousand dollar collection worth thirty-five. Patricia with her seventeen thousand dollars gone.

None of these people were foolish. All of them were impatient — with due diligence, with the learning required before buying, with the discipline of a systematic plan. The market exploited that impatience because the market always exploits impatience. That's what markets do.

You have something none of them had going in: the knowledge in this book. Use it slowly and deliberately. Make your first purchase a small one — not because you can't afford more, but because the habit of methodical, verified, well-priced buying is worth more than any individual transaction. Get comfortable with the process. Then build.

"Teaching Sarah the same lessons that protected our family's wealth. Real assets, fair prices, proper storage — knowledge she can use for life. The key is avoiding rare coin premiums and sticking with simple bullion. She's taking notes and asking smart questions. This wisdom will serve her family for generations."

THE LONG VIEW

Gold was real money for thousands of years before the modern financial system existed. It will almost certainly retain value long after whatever comes next. Silver has been used as currency on every inhabited continent, in every major civilization, across the entire span of recorded human history. These are not speculative assets chasing a trend. They are the oldest and most tested stores of value humanity has produced.

That historical durability doesn't mean prices only go up, or that there are no bad times to buy, or that precious metals replace the need for a complete financial plan. All of those caveats matter and this book has addressed them honestly. But it does mean that the fundamental case for owning some portion of your wealth in physical gold and silver — outside the banking system, outside the reach of inflation and currency debasement, tangible and universally recognized — is as sound today as it has ever been.

The financial system we live in is not permanent. No financial system in history has been permanent. The currencies we use are the most recent iteration of arrangements that have always eventually been revised, restructured, or replaced. Gold and silver have outlasted every one of them. They will almost certainly outlast the current ones.

That is not a prediction of imminent collapse or a case for fear. It's simply the historical record, observed plainly. And for buyers whose goal is preserving wealth across decades — through whatever the next financial cycle brings — the record provides a rational foundation for patient, disciplined accumulation of real assets.

Start where you are. Buy what you can afford to hold. Do it consistently, correctly, and without urgency. Protect what you accumulate. Document everything. And let time do what it has always done for patient holders of precious metals.

"Ten years of disciplined accumulation. We weathered market volatility, avoided scams, stored properly, and built real wealth outside the banking system. This Gold Eagle was my first purchase. Now I have a real portfolio protecting my family's future. Total invested: $60,000. Current value:

$95,000. Zero panic sales — held through volatility. The education, patience, and discipline were worth everything."

ONE FINAL THING

When I was starting out on Maxwell Street, an older dealer named Gus took me aside after I'd been there about a year. I'd made a few mistakes — nothing catastrophic, but enough to sting. He said something I've thought about hundreds of times since.

He said: the metals will take care of you if you take care of them. By which he meant: handle them right. Store them right. Buy them right. Don't let greed or fear make your decisions. Give them time. They'll do the rest.

Gus has been gone for decades. The metals are still here. So is the advice.

I hope this book has given you what you need to follow it.

James W. Bushnell

Florida, 2026

★ ***I own real assets, purchased wisely, protected properly, and held with patience. I am building wealth that lasts — for myself, and for the people I love.*** ★

PLAYBOOK BONUS

YOU'VE FINISHED THE PLAYBOOK

Download your free one-page PDF summary of the key information from this book—premium ranges, red flags, authentication tests, and buyer types at a glance.

Print it and reference it before every purchase.

Get your free guide:

www.valepublishing.com/playbook-bonus

READY TO GO DEEPER?

THE PRECIOUS METALS TRADE GUIDE

"Your Complete Encyclopedia of Advanced Precious Metals Knowledge"

You've learned the fundamentals. Now master the details...

This book gave you the essential knowledge to buy precious metals correctly — the buyer types, the products to choose, how to find legitimate dealers, fair pricing, authentication basics, and secure storage.

The Precious Metals Trade Guide takes you to the next level.

WHAT THE TRADE GUIDE COVERS:

- Two hundred pages of advanced techniques and detailed reference material
- Complete authentication protocols for every major bullion product
- Dealer evaluation frameworks used by professional buyers
- Advanced storage strategies for six-figure holdings
- Tax implications and reporting requirements
- Estate Planning for precious metals holdings
- Selling strategies that maximize recovery
- Market timing indicators (what actually works vs. noise)
- International buying and storage options
- Complete grading standards for numismatic coins
- Detailed product specifications and dimensions
- Red flag checklists for every transaction type

Think of this book as your foundation and the Trade Guide as the encyclopedia you reference when you need specific, detailed answers to advanced questions.

Ready to expand your knowledge?

Visit:
www.valepublishing.com/go/precious-metals-trade-guide.html

Or scan this QR code:

Thank you for reading. May your precious metals be acquired wisely, stored safely, and passed on for generations.

www.ingramcontent.com/pod-product-compliance
Lightning Source LLC
LaVergne TN
LVHW010624100826
845148LV00014B/3100